NEW
CONTAINER
ARCHITECTURE
DESIGN GUIDE + 30 CASE STUDIES

LINKS

NEW CONTAINER ARCHITECTURE: DESIGN GUIDE + 30 CASE STUDIES

© **LinksBooks 2013**
Jonqueres, 10, 1-5, Barcelona 08003, Spain
Tel.: +34-93-301-21-99
Fax: +34-93-301-00-21
info@linksbooks.net
ww.linksbooks.net

Author: Jure Kotnik
Compiled, edited & written: Jure Kotnik
Editorial coordination: Jacobo Krauel
Graphic design & production: Vid Brezočnik, graphic designer
Collaborator: Oriol Valles, graphic designer
English text translation: Biljana Božinovski

NEW CONTAINER ARCHITECTURE
DESIGN GUIDE + 30 CASE STUDIES

LINKS

CY

21

KR

LU

81460

2210

INTRODUCTION

CONTAINER ARCHITECTURE – A SUCCESS STORY

Container architecture is one of the youngest branches of architecture. It includes a variety of different-purpose different-typology different-outlook buildings that have at least one thing in common: the ISO container. Like Lego blocks, containers can be combined to create almost anything. They are perfect for temporary constructions, public buildings, family homes, event venues and everything in between. Container buildings have become popular with both architects and clients. They are easy to love, because they are quick to set up, low cost and eco-friendly as well as having status as art installations, and are therefore considered attractions in themselves. On the other hand, with more and more projects being realized, container architecture is increasingly gaining ground as a conventional branch of architecture: it is being chosen not so much for being "different" but for its advantages over other means of building, in cases where the budget is tight or deadlines short or when the terrain is very demanding. Architecture schools now teach students about containers, container solutions compete next to conventional projects at competitions, and world famous architects use them. Some projects even stand out as the peak architecture achievements of their time.

Container architecture has become a legitimate branch of architecture, being presented in books, magazines and at exhibitions.

Above: Container Architecture at NRW-Forum Düsseldorf, 2011.
Left: ESA Paris 2010.

Photo: Biljana Božinovski

At the world's first exhibition of container architecture in Ljubljana's Museum of Architecture and Design back in 2010, visitors assembled their own custom-made container constructions.

Photo: Kaja Brezočnik

EMERGING ARCHITECTURE:
CONTAINER ARCHITECTURE

The quality of container buildings and the increasing number of them emerging all over the world have established them as an integral part of architecture. The large number of award-winning, high quality projects around the globe leaves us in no doubt; buildings from containers have become an equal part of the architecture family. As with the other specific branches of architecture, container architecture has gained recognition and acclaim by being presented in books, at exhibitions and the online community. It is featured on many websites and social networks, and recently on a reality TV series Top Design on Australian Channel Nine. In this series, contestants had to transform a shipping container into an apartment.

Australia's Channel Nine broadcast the reality show Top Design, in which contestants had to transform a container into an apartment.

Photo: Channel Nine/MSN

Container Exhibition video

11

SYMBOL AND COCREATOR OF GLOBALIZATION

The ISO container is a steel box which has helped create globalized society as we know it. Odds are that practically everything we wear, sit on or even eat was brought to us from a distant part of the world in a container. The onset of globalization coincides with the boom of container transportation and it is safe to say we could not have one without the other. Today global transport depends to a large extent on containers. Containers travel the world on ships, trucks and the rail, transporting goods between distant parts of the globe. It is economically viable for companies to have branches in the Far East, where labour is much cheaper than in the West, and transport their goods to the Western markets by ship. Container shipping is the cheapest way to transport things: it costs only 14 euro cents to bring an iphone from China to Europe, which is close to nothing considering its market price.

There were ca. 29 million TEU (20' equivalent units) in the global transport chain in 2011 and the number is rising. As of 2009 approximately 90% of non-bulk cargo worldwide is moved by containers stacked on transport ships. In addition to being cheap, ocean shipping with containers leaves the smallest carbon footprint compared to other means of transportation: ocean transport produces fewer grams of exhaust gas emissions for each ton of cargo transported than air, rail, or road transport, as well as fewer particulate matter emissions. Once they have completed their journey, containers are recycled: as much as 98% of the entire container is recyclable.

Double-decker trains are increasing transport capacity.

Photo: Gregory Weirich

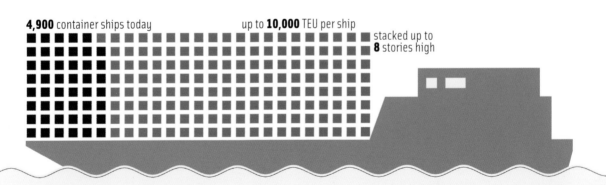

4,900 container ships today

up to **10,000** TEU per ship

stacked up to **8** stories high

12

Containers, neatly stacked in port and ready for loading onto ships.
Photo: Build IIc

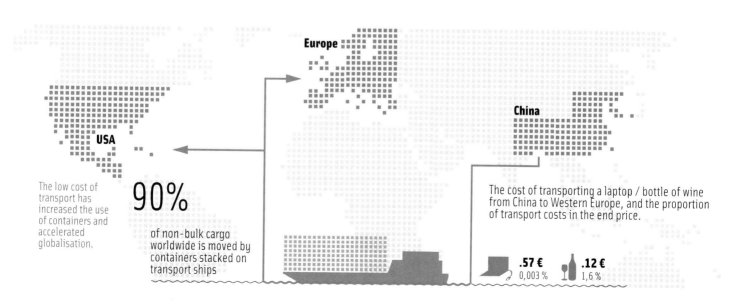

USA

Europe

China

The low cost of transport has increased the use of containers and accelerated globalisation.

90%

of non-bulk cargo worldwide is moved by containers stacked on transport ships

The cost of transporting a laptop / bottle of wine from China to Western Europe, and the proportion of transport costs in the end price.

.57 €
0,003 %

.12 €
1,6 %

THE HISTORY OF CONTAINERIZATION

The idea to use box-like structures to transport goods was born as soon as at the end of the 18th century in England to upgrade rail- and horse-drawn transport. The US government used small standard size container-boxes during the Second World War to upload as well as unload and distribute supplies; containers made this faster and more efficient. However, the real revolution started in 1955 with Malcom P. McLean. He was a trucking entrepreneur from North Carolina, USA, who had bought a steamship company and came up with the idea of loading entire truck trailers onto ships, with their cargo still inside. He realized it is much simpler and quicker to lift a container full of goods from a vehicle and load it directly onto a ship, as opposed to loading cargo in smaller chunks. This gave birth to so-called intermodalism, i.e. the system of transportation where two or more modes of transport are combined to simplify and speed up the flow of (people and) goods. The same container with the same cargo could now be transported with minimum interruption via different transport modes – with ship, truck and train. This simplified the logistical process and lead to a revolution in cargo transportation and international trade, and many years later entered the field of architecture.

Malcolm P. Mclean, a trucking entrepreneur and the father of the shipping container as we know it today.

Photo:Maersk

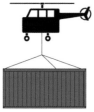

The containers' main advantage is their intermodality--the fact that they can move from one means of transport to another without their contents being unloaded and reloaded.

SIZES AND TYPES

Intermodal containers ("intermodal" implies that they can be moved from one mode of transport to another without unloading and reloading their contents) can be used for a variety of purposes and are accordingly known under numerous names. "Standardized" containers are those that comply with ISO standards stipulating length, width, height, capacity. Container capacity is often expressed in twenty-foot equivalent units or TEU, which is a measure of containerized cargo capacity equal to one standard 20' by 8' container. In addition to the most common dry-cargo shipping containers, containers are also used to transport perishable goods (refrigerated containers), boats, vehicles, machinery or industrial equipment (flat-rack containers), vegetables such as onions and potatoes (open side containers), bulk minerals and heavy machinery (open top bulktainers), bulk liquids such as wine, vegetable oil and chemicals (tank containers). Garmentainers are used to ship garments on hangers, half-height containers for dense products. All these containers are built to the same exterior lengths and widths as the standard dry cargo containers. Every container has its own unique unit number, often called a box number, which can be used by ship captains, coastguards, dock supervisors, customs officers and warehouse managers to identify who owns the container, who is using it to ship goods, and even track its whereabouts anywhere in the world.

There is another kind of containers: a kind that is intermodal and the same size as the others but not meant to transport goods. Building containers are designed for the direct use in the construction industry and are mainly used as office or housing accommodation.

Containers exist in various shapes and sizes, fitting the various transportation requirements.

tank container

		20' container		40' container		45' high-cube container	
		imperial	metric	imperial	metric	imperial	metric
external dimensions	length	19' 10"	6.058 m	40' 0"	12.192 m	45' 0"	13.716 m
	width	8' 0"	2.438 m	8' 0"	2.438 m	8' 0"	2.438 m
	height	8' 6"	2.591 m	8' 6"	2.591 m	9' 6"	2.896 m
interior dimensions	length	18' 10 5/16"	5.758 m	39'5 45/64"	12.032 m	44' 4"	13.556 m
	width	7'8 8 19/32"	2.352 m	7'8 19/32"	2.352 m	7' 8 19/32"	2.352 m
volume		1,169 ft³	33.1 m³	2,385 ft³	67.5 m³	3,040 ft³	86.1 m³
maximum gross mass		52.910 lb	24,000 kg	37,200 lb	30,480 kg	67,200 lb	30,480 kg
net load		48,060 lb	21,800 kg	58,820 lb	26,680 kg	56,620 lb	25,680 kg
area	exterior	158,972 sq ft	14,769 m²	339,041 sq ft	31,498 m²	359,934 sq ft	33,439 kg
	interior	145,764 sq ft	13,542 m²	304,607 sq ft	28,299 m²	343,185 sq ft	31,883 kg

flat-rack
container

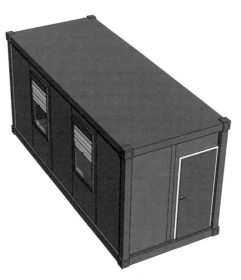

building
container

cargo shipping
container

open top
container

open side
container

refrigerated
container

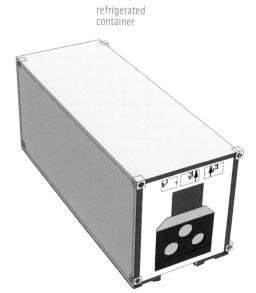

BUILDING CONTAINERS

Building containers are the type of ISO containers most frequently used in architecture, as well as dry-cargo shipping containers. They existed even before the container architecture that we know today came into being, emerging through the transformation of shipping containers. Modular building containers were originally seen as products rather than being considered architecture. Their primary purpose is to create functional buildings, leaving architecture as such largely unarticulated. Recently there have been improvements in this area too, mainly on account of the advances in container architecture in general. Building containers are becoming increasingly interesting and have to date been used by renowned architects such as MVRDV (Center for Cancer Studies), HVDN (Qubic Student Housing), Jean Nouvel (Wismar Technology), etc.

The main difference between a shipping container and building container is the construction frame. Building containers have weaker frames as they are meant to stack to a maximum three levels which, considering a single unit is the most common type of container structure, is significant. The frame is not fixed but must be assembled, and the insulated façade is not a single piece but has several segments that are put together on site. Façade segments may include windows and doors. Joints and welding are similar to the ones of other standardised ISO containers. Building containers are therefore optimized for office/housing purposes and take even less time to set up than converted shipping containers. Their major advantages are the fact that they are perfectly compatible with the transport system and that they facilitate speedy and low-cost construction. Downsides include the fact that they are manufactured for use in the construction industry, rather than recycled.

MOBILE

TEMPORARY

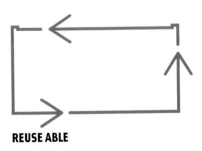

REUSE ABLE

Building containers provide fast and cost effective housing solutions, frequently used for student accommodation (Amsterdam, Holland).

Building containers are also efficient for solving spatial problems in public buildings. The temporary kindergarten Ajda by Arhitektura Jure Kotnik was used for one year and then recycled.

Photo:Kitch-Nitch, Vid Brezočnik

Building containers represent ready-made living space and are easily stacked. They are also low cost, but unfortunately often to the detriment of architecture.

Photo:Euromodul.hr

WHAT MAKES CONTAINERS CONVENIENT FOR ARCHITECTURE?

Containers are prefabricated, mass-produced, mobile and intermodal (they can switch means of transport such as ship, truck, rail). They are easily accessible all around the world. They are sturdy and resistant, durable and stackable, as well as being modular, recyclable and reusable. They constitute a space/room in themselves, and have a steel frame that can support the entire structure. Container buildings are quick to assemble on site and withstand the worst weather conditions: cold and heat, as well as salt water, high wind, heavy rain and other inconveniences. Container constructions are not necessarily fixed in size and can grow together with the needs of their tenants: if a family or office needs more space, additional containers can be added to enlarge the existing structure at any time. Likewise, containers can be removed to downsize a space. Containers are also relatively cheap, a used one costing as little as $1,500 on average, while the price for a new one is ca. $4,000. Using shipping containers for buildings requires a much smaller budget than conventional construction methods, which makes container architecture accessible even to those with tight budgets.

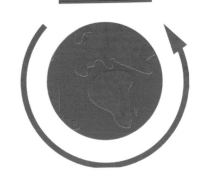

Containers are easily accessible all around the world. They are sturdy and resistant, durable and stackable. They are modular, recyclable and reusable.

Containers are prefabricated, mass-produced, mobile and can be assembled into buildings very fast.

Containers can withstand the worst of weather conditions: the cold and the heat as well as salty water, high winds, downpours and other inconveniences.

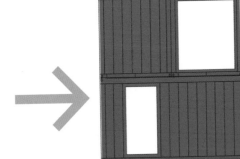

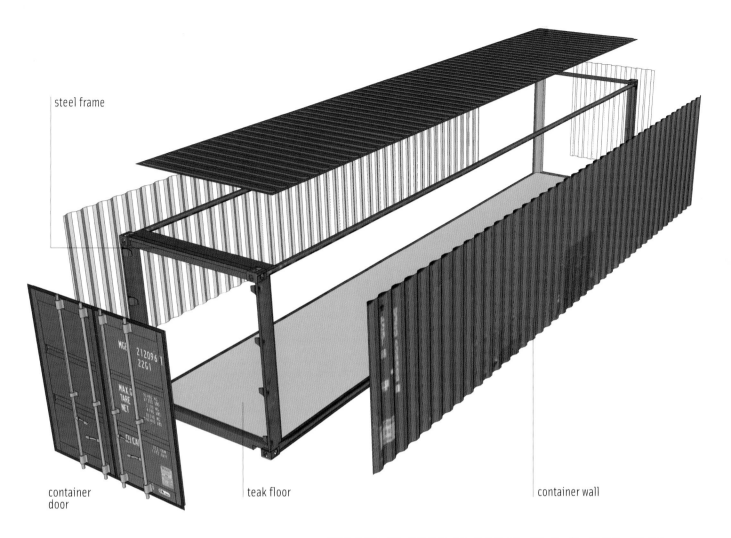

steel frame

container door

teak floor

container wall

THE BUILDING BLOCK OF CONTAINER ARCHITECTURE

Containers are mod-
ules consisting
of a steel framework,
thin plate outer shell
and roof, and mainly
wooden floors on a
steel base. Being
rectangular solids
they are ready-made
spaces as it is, and
can become interest-
ing architecture
material with just a
few simple touches.

Containers are the elementary building blocks of container architecture, to which they also give its name. The noun container derives from the verb "to contain" and accurately denotes the containers' primary function: to hold (and transport) goods. Containers are modules consisting of a steel framework, thin plate outer shell and roof, and mainly wooden floors on a steel base. Being rectangular solids they are ready-made spaces as it is, and can become interesting architecture material with just a few simple touches. The elementary container construction is twice as solid as that required by any building code, which makes it appropriate as a building block even without modifications. Containers are also hurricane, flood, and earthquake-resistant (due to being lightweight), they are fire-proof (thanks to the special thin plate coating), weather proof and successfully fight other inconveniences (such as rodent problems). Despite sharing the same elementary base, container architecture projects are not monotonous. Containers are building blocks, which, like brick, can be used to create a variety of different-purpose different-outlook constructions.

OPTIMIZING THE SYSTEM

Containers first appeared as a tool for optimising the transport chain. The next step was ISO standards, which created a system of identical dimensions in containers worldwide. But transport has changed over time, calling for new optimizations. Given their vast impact on global trade, even the smallest improvements made on containers can save millions, especially considering the world trade imbalance, which results in empty containers traveling from the West to the East.

Shipping containers have not changed much over time, but there have been tendencies to increase their size, especially in countries with wide roads, such as the USA and Australia. One such ISO compliant upgrade is the 45' container with just over 10% more in length than its 40' counterpart. Several types exist but the most common is the 45 high cube, which is 9.6' tall. Other upgrades include collapsible containers and those made not from steel but other, lighter and eco-friendlier materials. An example is Cargoshell, a shipping container which collapses when empty to a quarter of its full size in just 30 seconds. It is made of a composite material that weighs 25% less than standard shipping containers, which lightens its carbon footprint even further (less fossil fuel is required to transport and manipulate it). George Kochanowski took optimization to a new level by creating the Staxxon system, which uses vertical folding to diminish an empty container to 20% of its original size, so that five empty containers can be transported in place of a single unfolded one. Even before such adaptations appeared on shipping containers they were introduced on building containers with the Transpack system. It collapses building containers into flat-packs that take up one-fourth of the space of an assembled unit, so that four units can be transported for the price of one. Perhaps the same rationale will spread to container architecture as well, so that container buildings can change volume as required; the space around the core of the building can be expanded or minimized, causing higher or lower maintenance costs, and similar.

A flatpack container is a building container optimised to save space when empty, taking up one fourth of the space of an assembled unit, so that four units can be transported for the price of one.

Photo:Euromodul.hr

Flatpack assembly video

Staxxon Video

The Staxxon system uses vertical folding to diminish an empty container to 20% of its original size, so that five empty containers can be transported in place of a single unfolded one.

Collapsing empty containers like Staxxon could help reduce the costs of transporting the numerous empty containers in the West back to the East.

Photo: Staxxon.com

Flexotels units are hotel rooms based on ISO containers, which can be quickly and easily assembled and disassembled.

Photo: Flexotels.com

EVOLUTION OF CONTAINER ARCHITECTURE

Container architecture has witnessed a bottom-up development, with architects joining late in the process. The compact and sturdy transport box which is weather-, fire- and earthquake-resistant and which defies several other types of inconveniences naturally lent itself to experimental use. Containers thus spontaneously became shacks, stores and shelters, particularly in third world countries. The first container architecture projects in the West were statements and manifestos showing that a single container is enough to create a living space. Custom-made interiors facilitates diverse functions within a minimal space. Early upgrades included adding extra space to a single container, usually by installing hydraulic fittings which lifted its sides to expand the interior outwards. The LOT-EK Mobile Dwelling Unit is designed in this vein, with extruded sub-volumes increasing living space when in use and pushed back inside during transport.

The next stages of development included stacking several containers into larger formations, where intermediate walls could be removed to create large open interior spaces. After that containers were combined with other construction materials, resulting in more dynamic projects and larger and higher quality living/working spaces. A few of the most brilliant container villas, such as the 12 Container House, Redondo Beach House and Chalet du Chemin Brochu, are from this period. The trend which followed after placed other materials, such as wood, on top of the outer shell of the container. The conventional exterior appearance robbed container architecture of some of its essence but made it more widely acceptable to the public and attracted a wider range of clients.

Today container projects are no longer limited to innovative architects but are also becoming established as a commercially viable branch of modular architecture. They copy mass produced modular buildings in function as well as form and are often lacking in architectural articulation. This sort of differentiation in terms of quality is in keeping with all other major branches of architecture, resulting in a large number of container projects but only a very small proportion of outstanding ones.

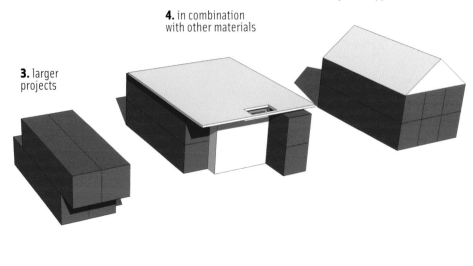

1. conceptual use

2. expanding space (hydraulics)

3. larger projects

4. in combination with other materials

5. standard prefab approach

In the past twenty years container architecture has had several stages of development.

Pioneer projects used a single container at first, but soon the tendency to expand the interior appeared. Mobile Dwelling Unit by LOT-EK, 2001.

Photo: LOT-EK

Combining containers with other materials gave container architecture new momentum, resulting in several cover architecture projects. Redondo Beach House by De Maria Design, 2007.

Recently containers have started appearing in projects for the standard real estate market. They are used for the construction, which is concealed by the facade. Photo: batiloc.fr

Photo: Andre Movsesyan

THE RISE OF CONTAINER ARCHITECTURE

Container architecture is popular, in-demand, and ever-more frequent in the modern world. According to the Intermodal Steel Building Units and Container Homes Association, shipping-container based construction is currently one of the fastest growing building trends, particularly in the United States. At first container architecture appealed mainly to people in the design, fashion and architecture worlds, while in recent years more and more people from all walks of life are beginning to appreciate containers' trendy image. Container projects are rewarding: architects like them because they receive a great deal of media coverage, home owners are delighted because container homes meet their expectations of a cosmopolitan and eco-friendly home, and companies are happy because container offices and shops make good advertising, and are practical and mobile. Companies can tug their shops along on trucks and open them at various locations, even the most prestigious ones, at the flick of a switch. Everybody involved benefits from the quick set up, low cost and flexibility.

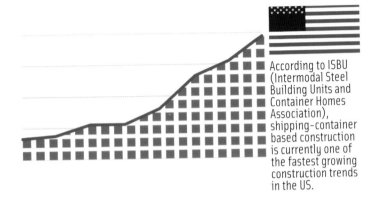

According to ISBU (Intermodal Steel Building Units and Container Homes Association), shipping-container based construction is currently one of the fastest growing construction trends in the US.

The wide publicity given to container projects by the media has made it increasingly popular with both clients and architects.

Container architecture is most likely the most awarded branch of architecture, considering the number of projects built and the number of awards received.

Photo: psdGraphic

AWARD WINNING ARCHITECTURE

The fact that container buildings offer fast and high quality solutions for many of the pressing problems of the world today, as well as their fresh approach and trendy character, seem to convince judging panels to hand architecture awards to container projects. Container architecture is likely the most awarded branch of architecture, considering the number of projects built and the number of awards received. Conceptual projects and student designs have also received numerous awards. This reflects the wide scope of uses containers can be put to in architecture as well as the "right time-right place" aspect to the work. The list of award winning container architecture projects is long and impressive. Several of the buildings in this book have won awards, while others, especially the most recent projects, may still receive their due acclaim.

SUPERSTAR CLIENTS AND SUPERSTAR ARCHITECTS

One glimpse at the list of corporate clients that have commissioned architects to construct container structures for them reveals that this must be a winning recipe. Established brand names did not choose container architecture by chance, they chose it for its numerous advantages. The well known companies that have included containers into their various marketing or other campaigns include Puma, Adidas, Nike, Rolex, Ikea, Tommy Hilfiger, UniQLO, LEGO, Illy, Starbucks, Volvo and others. On the other side of the equation, container projects are being delivered by a diverse company of architects, from young emerging designers to architecture superstars. The latter include renowned names like Shigeru Ban (Papertainer Museum in Seoul, Nomadic Museum in New York), Jean Nouvel (Wismar Technology and Research Center in Wismar), MVRDV (Cancer Center in Amsterdam), Will Alsop (Fawood Children's Centre) and others. Container architecture has been right on trend for some time now, and has served as a breakthrough form for several architects who have won early-career international acclaim building with containers.

In designing the Fawood Children's Centre in London, Will Alsop protected the container-based structure with a roof to enable outdoor play all year round despite the British weather.

Photo: Roderick Coyne, Alan Lai

Hotaï Village, an alternative approach to tourism, supporting social and ecological awareness in Senegal. Designed by French designer Matali Crasset.

Photo: Benjamin Bonnell

Push Button House by Adam Kalkin, serving Illy coffee in the function of a temporary cafe in Venice.

Photo: Illlycaffe S.A.

In Tukwila, Washington, Starbucks have set up a recycled shipping container drive-thru coffee shop.

Photo:Tom Ackerman, Starbucks

In designing the VOLVO C30 Experience, the Stockholm-based KNOCK created a contrasting environment with old containers used for the background.

Photo: Mikael Olsson

ARCHITECTURE OF INNOVATIVE SOCIETIES

Container architecture is closely associated with advanced, flexible and open societies. The keynote speaker at the world's first ever container architecture exhibition, which opened in 2009 in Ljubljana, Slovenia, Professor Janez Koželj asserted that container architecture has emerged most strongly and is especially popular in technologically advanced countries that support creativity, especially if it helps to solve social problems. Such countries include the United States, Japan, the Netherlands, South Korea, Germany, the UK, France, Switzerland, and many other developed nations. Container architecture is a challenge for innovative architects and skilful designers to promoting and push forward the inquiring nature of architecture. Recycling shipping containers and making use of a series of other sustainable-construction features, container architecture fits well into the contemporary green-minded society and is a constituent part of the upcoming post-contemporary architecture.

Co Containers

Ar Architecture

Su Sustainability

In Innovative use

Container architecture has emerged most strongly and is especially popular in technologically advanced countries that support creativity.

Photo: Brammo.com

CONTAINER
ARCHITECTURE TYPOLOGY

Container architecture is an open code construction system and can be used to build practically anything. Found in virtually all developed environments, container buildings differ primarily with respect to their size, purpose and typology. As to their typology, container projects are either standalone units or extensions of existing buildings. They may involve a single container or several combined into a compound, perhaps involving additional construction materials (mixed constructions). They may serve to add spice to conventional buildings, or to solve rooftop issues and complement the interiors of buildings.

Most common container architecture types

rooftop container

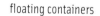

mixed structure

container extension

container compound

single container

use in the interior

container spice-up

floating containers

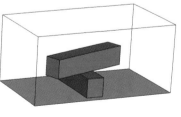

A SINGLE CONTAINER

Statistically the largest number of container architecture projects involve a single container. Single container structures seem to be the most popular, while structures with larger numbers of containers are fewer: the larger the number of containers involved, the smaller the number of realized projects. Single container projects are especially popular with conceptual work, brand promotion and small events, as a single container is usually enough to promote a message. One container is large enough to fit a bar, small restaurant, shop or office. It is mobile, inexpensive and often does not require a building permit. The latter is an important asset as it significantly cuts the related red tape. Single container units can be standalone or attached to a building. If, for instance, a music room, sauna, guest house etc is required, it can be set up in a container and easily fit it into a back garden. Single container units are often used as retreat cabins in rural areas and in tourism, but they are also popular in top spot urban locations for various promotional campaigns.

Future Shack, one of the first container based projects, created in the 1990s. By Sean Godsell.
Photo: Earl Carter

Single containers are often used in conceptual projects, such as Damien Chivialle's Urban Farm.
Photo: Damien Chivialle

Kunsthalle by Platoon and Graft architects is a compound from 28 containers and hosts a booming cultural centre in Seoul.

Photo:Platoon.org

The Riverside Building, the third of the Container City projects, is a compound made of 73 containers, hosting offices and apartments on the banks of the River Thames.

Photo:Sarah Hewson/Containercity

CONTAINER COMPOUNDS

While a single container unit is perfectly suitable for a number of purposes, sometimes one container is just not big enough. Moreover, a single container is limiting to a long and narrow distribution of space, which can be awkward. Luckily, containers can easily be stacked together into compounds. Depending on what is needed, an unlimited number of containers can be put together. For a holiday home 2 might suffice, for an office building perhaps 15, for a mall 60 or more. As far as the size of container compounds goes, the sky is the limit, which means that that the possible uses are practically unlimited.

If shipping containers are to be stacked together into a compound, they need to be properly prepped, while building containers are ready made for compounding. This is why ISO building containers are often used to construct large buildings, such as barracks, schools, kindergartens, and office buildings.

BUILDING EXTENSIONS

Containers are a fast and efficient tool to expand existing buildings. They can add more room to existing programmes or introduce new content, are a handy solution because they cause minimum site impact, involve low noise pollution and function according to the plug and play principles. Containers are a very sensible solution for adding space because they can easily be dismantled and recycled again should the need pass.

This area of container architecture has great potential. Perhaps in the future home-owners will order specialized custom-made top brand container accessories from online catalogues, such as a Whirlpool wellness centre, an Apple multimedia room, a Nike fitness module and so on. Jones and Partners have pointed their finger in the same direction with their Package Home Tower. Judging from Charles Nogry's House Extension in Nantes, which we are publishing in this volume, all this is slowly becoming reality.

Container extensions are a simple way of adding space to the existing structure.
Photo: Stephane Chalmeau

A temporary container extension can help solve shortages of space in kindergartens.

MIXED CONSTRUCTIONS AND SPICE-UPS

Containers are certainly convenient and versatile; however, they do not offer a universal solution to every problem. Container architecture reaches a completely new level of potential when complemented with other construction materials such as wood, steel and concrete. This is particularly important for integrating containers into sloping terrain: most times concrete slabs will be used to even out the slope and containers are placed on top. Exterior cladding also helps improve container performance: timber slats, for instance, help protect them from overheating. Additional constructions can be used to support containers, lift them from the ground or set them apart to create large open spaces between them (cf. Manifesto House on p. 66 and the 12 Container House by Adam Kalkin).

Sometimes architects and/or clients want to use containers not for the supporting structures, i.e. not to "build" something, but to spice things up and add additional flavour to their story. In such cases containers are usually statements in themselves.

Container architecture hits a completely new level of potential when complemented with other construction materials such as wood, steel and concrete.

Photo: Normand Rajotte

The UniQlo container in Tokyo as a three-fold spice-up: entrance box, projecting roof, and changing cabins on the first floor. By LOT-EK.

Photo: Danny Bright

ROOFTOPS

Containers are also frequently used on rooftops. Their light-weight construction and simple set up are their key advantages when it comes to finding solutions for a penthouse or rooftop office. Containers require no special foundations and can easily be attached to a flat roof, therefore their set up is fast and does not interfere with the life in the building below. Jean Nouvel and Ziebell+ Partner used containers in such a way to spread the offices of the Wismar Technology Center onto the roof at their location in Wismar. They also increase the opportuniy of owning a loft in downtown New York when all conventional places are taken! The Guzman Penthouse by LOT-EK is a container-made penthouse on a rooftop close to the Empire State Building.

Their light weight allows containers to be placed on the roofs of existing buildings. Guzman's penthouse by LOT-EK on a rooftop close to the Empire State Building, NY.

Photos: Paul Warchol

Photos:Containercity.com

Containers are
lightweight and
easy to mount
on prefabricated
pontoons. London
Container City's
floating containers.

FLOATING
CONTAINERS

Mounted on pontoons, containers can be used to create floating buildings. This is a popular and attractive choice of housing in countries where regulations governing vessels are looser than those governing construction on land. In addition, floating containers in such cases can take advantage of top spot locations along river banks, lake shorelines and the sea coastline where building is not permitted. Pontoon containers are therefore not only used for coastal and shoreline infrastructure but housing as well. Containers are lightweight and easy to mount on prefabricated pontoons. If the pontoon is large enough, the front (or back) section can function as a terrace.

INTERIORS
WITH CONTAINERS

Containers are being increasingly used for interior solutions as well. Of course, the room which houses a container must be tall enough, and for this very banal reason containers are usually used inside public buildings more than inside homes, although the latter also happens. They function as a special place inside a larger space, hosting an additional programme, functioning as a pavilion. They are useful for large open office buildings, because they have a cosmopolitan air about them and create a globetrotting atmosphere, and because they offer small enclosures that can be turned into a kitchenette, xerox room, relaxation room, a room for meetings, etc. Such offices are cool to work in, and are commissioned by companies with open-minded CEOs. Flip to p. 85 to check out the cool office created and used by Group 8, and go to page 119 to take a look at the inspiring loft of the Wardell&Sagan family, which brought into their home two shipping containers that serve a practical purpose as well as complement the owner's collection of contemporary art.

With their cosmopolitan spirit, containers can spice up the inside of a home. (Wardell Sagan Projekt)

Photo:Drew Kelly

A king size "interior" container project: Temporary event stage inside the Paris Grand Palais. By 1024 architecture and Cedric Denoyel.

Photo: Cedric Denoyel

Video: Setting up the container event stage in Paris Grand Palais.

Containers
can function
as thematic
pavilions
inside a vast
open interior.
Cargo offices
by Group 8.

Photo: Regis Golay

CONTAINER ARCHITECTURE IN USE

Containers can be used in most kinds of architecture. Theoretically, container-based projects can be divided into three categories: public buildings, housing and event architecture. Practically they are being used to create a vast range of structures from kindergartens to bars and restaurants to churches, garages, theatres, lighthouses, emergency hurricane shelters. Other uses have included concession stands, fire and military training facilities, emergency shelters, weekend houses, villas, student housing, retirement homes, motels and hotels, apartment and office buildings, art studios, shops, bank vaults, medical clinics, radar stations, shopping malls, guest rooms, recording studios, abstract art, mobile factories, experimental labs, farming gardens, bathrooms and showers, workshops, construction trailers, mine site accommodations, exploration camps, technology and research centres, event stages, concert viewing decks, bus stations, cruise centres and so on. Clearly the possibilities for container use are near-endless.

Containers are popular for restaurants, such as Rotterdam's Wijn of Water by Bijvoet architektuur.

Photo: Maarten Laupman

Probably the most famous toilets in the world. AFF's International Youth Center Barleber See has made it into some of the most distinguished selections of contemporary architecture.

Photo: AFF architekten

Like giant Lego blocks, containers can be combined to create almost anything.

Photo: LEGO

Easy to assemble, easy to dismantle: containers are frequent companions of music festivals. Nuit Sonores in Lyon by Looking for architecture and Cedric Denoyel (RCS).

Photo: Denis Chaussende

PUBLIC BUILDINGS

Throughout history public buildings have had a very special place in every community. They typically differ from other buildings in size, appearance and the materials used to construct them. At first sight containers may appear ill-suited for use in public buildings such as hospitals or nurseries; however, the many existing top quality container-based public buildings prove otherwise. Clever architecture and carefully chosen details have often been combined with containers to create public buildings that rest on sound conceptual foundations as well as wear a specific aesthetics. Since containers are relatively cheap to build with, it is easy enough to create very large buildings with them – that is, if lots of space is what we are looking for. An example of a monumental building constructed from containers is Shigeru Ban's Nomadic Museum. It is made entirely from recycled materials: containers are used for the frame structure, cardboard for the colonnade. The magnificent ambience of the Nomadic Museum has nothing to envy the atmosphere of a traditional building. Containers are also useful for temporary installations of public space as they can afterwards be taken apart and recycled.

Containers have also been cleverly used to create larger public buildings, usually built from other construction materials. Papertainer Museum by Shigeru Ban.

Photo: Jongoh Kim Designhouse

The temporary Cruise Center in the Port of Hamburg by RHW Architekten is made from containers, the spacious hall being covered with a magical illuminated roof.

Photo: Christoph Grebler

Containers can accommodate dynamic start-up centers (AAS de Santiago, Galicia, Spain).

Photo: AAS archive

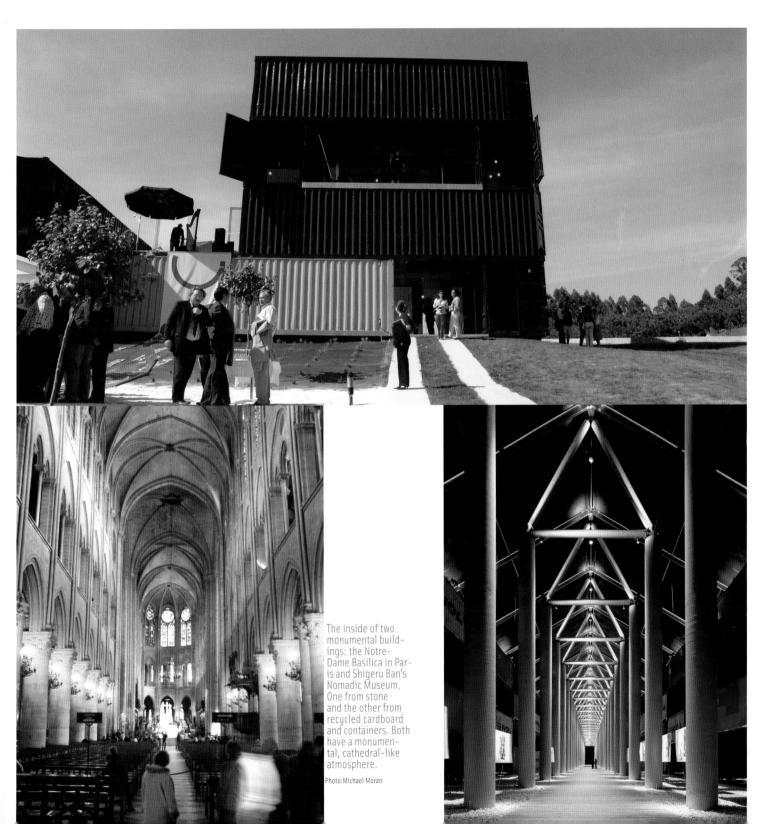

The inside of two monumental buildings: the Notre-Dame Basilica in Paris and Shigeru Ban's Nomadic Museum. One from stone and the other from recycled cardboard and containers. Both have a monumental, cathedral-like atmosphere.

Photo: Michael Moran

HOUSING PROJECTS

Containers can be used for a wide variety of housing solutions, from small-scale cabins to container villas and large apartment buildings. At first architects used containers to try and fit an entire apartment into them. These were the initial artistic and experimental projects designed for the so-called urban nomads, the 'side-products' of the modern society. Gradually architects and designers recognized containers as useful for holiday cabins, but it took quite a while for the general public to find them appealing too. Today containers as a building block are being combined with other construction materials to create homes increasingly similar to other prefabs. Single family homes are still largely client-oriented and custom made but serial prefabs based on containers are also available on the market. The construction of larger container-made apartment buildings is driven mainly by their practical value and economic efficiency, both for investors and users. The largest container-made apartment buildings contain as many as 1,000 units (e.g. student housing Qubic in Amsterdam). The modular monotony of such a vast number of identical elements can be broken down by diverse façades and installation patterns.

This family home in the Spanish village El Tiemblo by James and Mau architects is made entirely from reused / recycled materials.

Photo: Pablo Sarabia

Amsterdam's Qubic is a container-based student housing project by HVDN architekten.

Photo:Luuk Kramer

Container apartments are
spacious, bright and high
quality. Riverside Building
by ABK architects.

Photo:Containercity.com

EVENT ARCHITECTURE

Containers seem the perfect solution for event architecture. They are trendy and unusual and can be combined in a variety of ways to represent an event as well and as specifically as possible. Another huge advantage is the fact that they are mobile, which makes it possible for an event venue to easily move location or be put away for storing when not in use. Because containers leave a site practically intact and can be taken apart in no time, they are perfect for temporary constructions and can be set up practically anywhere, including in in-demand urban locations. This adds to the scope for creativity, and consequently the appeal of a particular event. Sometimes a single container is used, sometimes over a hundred, configured to respond specifically to the needs of the particular event.

Container Bar video

This container aqueduct functioned as a mobile gallery and stage, promoting the 2008 Expo in Zaragoza.
Photo: BOPBAA archive

The ICON by Spillmann/ Felser was a red container compound in the form of the Swiss cross, promoting the Euro 2008 in Switzerland.
Photo: Swiss tourism

One of the main advantages of container architecture is the possibility to set it up in top locations. ICON in Dam Square, Amsterdam.

Seen on many occasions at various events: container-based mobile bars. (by Looking for architecture and Cedric Denoyel (RCS)).
Photo: Mathieu Despeysses

SUSTAINABILITY OF CONTAINER ARCHITECTURE

We live in the times of strong focus on the environment, and containers can accommodate a large number of ecological features we want in buildings. First of all, they can be recycled and reused, and they reduce the amount of other construction materials used. This makes container architecture comply with the 3R design concept (reuse, recycle, reduce). Container constructions usually call for no preliminary groundwork, which further reduces site impact, and are quick to set up, which means less noise pollution and less waste on the construction site. A smaller container construction can be fully erected within a single day, while larger structures may take up to several days. Many container projects, most notably the smaller or conceptual ones, strive towards being energy self-sufficient and off-grid by using solar panels, rainwater collectors, green roofs, etc. Interiors are also often environment-friendly, being furnished in timber and other natural or recycled materials.

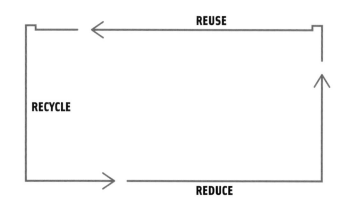

The cargotecture c192 Nomad by HyBrid Architecture uses a recycled container and combines it with various sustainable technologies. Also available in the off-grid version.

Photo: HyBridarc.com

The Futuro House by the Finnish architect Matti Suuronen. Less than 100 versions of this legendary prefab were actually built.

Photo: happyfamousartists.blogspot.fr

The prefab market is defined by the triangle price – design – acceptability for the market.

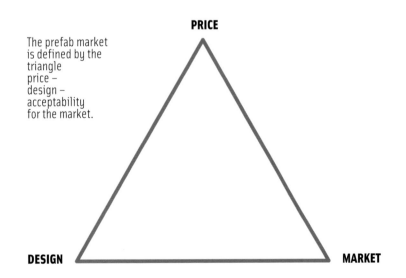

PRICE

DESIGN

MARKET

WHY CONTAINERS AND NOT OTHER PREFABS?

Architects have long attempted to come up with cost-efficient architecture that is easy to transport, modular and prefabricated. Most attempts are unsuccessful, as the projects are overdesigned or too revolutionary for the time or they address too small a group of potential clients. These factors prevent mass production, raise costs and diminishes the market for such projects.

Containers, on the other hand, have none of these problems. They are present as it is, being a by-product of the world trade and transport chain, they are cheap, easy to transport and as prefabricated as it gets. They are available everywhere and anywhere. Moreover, they are recyclable and reusable: if a building is no longer needed, containers can be taken apart and put to different uses.

A NICHE OR IS THERE MORE?

Container architecture has become an established branch of architecture, but is it a real alternative to other construction approaches or merely a niche that adds interest to the prefab market? The calculation is rather simple. The World Shipping Council has estimated that 29.2 million TEU (20' equivalent units) were in use in 2011. This equals a total of 429.3 million square meters of container material. On the other end of the equation are the 2 billion square meters of new developments, which is roughly the annual growth rate of the construction market in China according to Prof. Wang Wei of the Shanghai Research Institute of Building Sciences. Even if all the world's shipping containers (dry freight special and standard, tank, refrigerators) were pulled from the transport chain and converted into buildings, they could only service China's construction market for a period of about 78 days. There are therefore not enough containers available to significantly change trends in architecture. Even in the best case scenario with maximum utilization of existing containers, container architecture could never play a high-profile role on the global construction market. In certain niche areas, however, such as modular prefabricated buildings, temporary housing or event architecture, containers do present themselves as the best alternative.

All world's shipping containers (dry freight special and standard, tank, refrigerators) could service China's real-estate market for 78 days only.

78 days

■ **29,1** mio TEU in 2011

1 2 3 4 5 6 7 8 9 10 11
weeks

CONTAINER ARCHITECTURE GUIDELINES

FORMING SPACES

There are two main ways in which a container building can be structured, depending on the desired position of containers in relation to each other. Units can either be stacked close together into an indivisible whole, or set apart to create open spaces between them. The former approach is often used for simpler projects, especially those that will eventually be moved, with the downside being double construction patterns. The latter approach is used to create a more diverse floor plan and include other construction materials, such as steel or wood. Fewer containers are needed to create the same interior surface. The main disadvantage of this approach is that it strips the building of mobility – one of containers' main features.

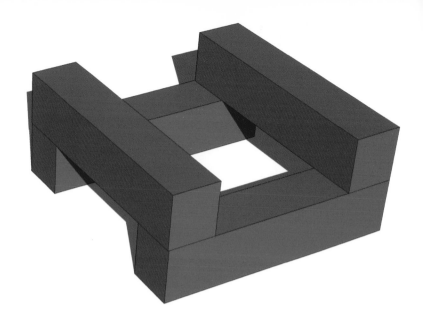

Creating spaces in between containers.

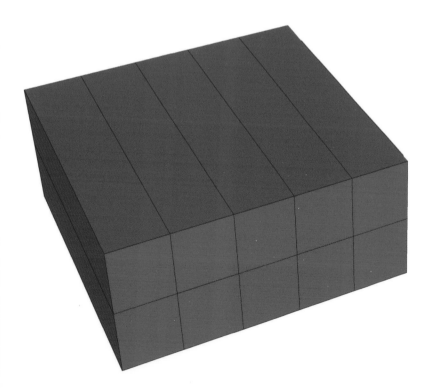

Creating spaces with containers one next to the other.

STACKING

The containers' steel frame is intended for elementary stacking, one on top of the other. This is quick and easy but can result in boring and monotonous buildings. Nonetheless, the spatial potential of container architecture is endless and appealing structures are only a matter of creativity and imagination. With proper static reinforcement, containers can be stacked and combined with other materials in any number of ways to create out-of-the-box innovative systems buildings.

Containers stacked in dynamic compositions create eye catching structures but usually require additional static reinforcement.

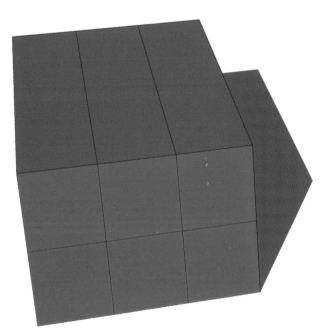

Stacking containers one on top of the other.

THE OUTSIDE LOOK

One consideration in finishing a container building is its final outwards appearance. The nature of the structure can be left to show or hidden behind a façade. Early container buildings tended to leave the containers as they were, and today the industrial look is often preserved as a statement in itself, revealing the containers' hip cosmopolitan origin. The corrugated thin plate has all the characteristics of a façade anyway and this drives down costs, as most of the budget can be used to shape up the interior. However, there are also a number of innovatiove alternatives for disguising the container exterior.

Containers are compatible with a variety of materials today, so clients can choose practically any façade they want. This is an important momentum for container architecture, as "the usual" façades make container buildings acceptable to a much larger market. Sometimes containers are covered with an additional skin because of insulation: if there is insufficient room for insulation inside, it must be added on the outside and is usually covered with a further protective outer shell.

Container look   or   secondary façade cover

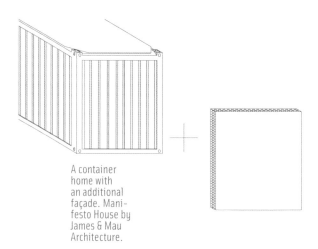

A container home with an additional façade. Manifesto House by James & Mau Architecture.

Photo: Antonio Corcuera

Many container projects use stickers to create a graphic expression on the façade. 2+ weekend house by Jure Kotnik.

Photo: Vid Brezočnik

The outside of a container home can be industrial and rough, showing the true container nature of the building. El Tiemblo House by James & Mau Architecture.

Photo: Pablo Sarabia

APPROPRIATE USE

The use of containers in architecture should be carefully considered on a case by case basis. They constitute a good solution for projects that highlight their best features such as mobility, intermodality, lightness, easy assembly, low price and low site impact, etc. It is especially their mobility that puts them at an advantage over other constructions, therefore they are particularly well suited for temporary buildings and event architecture, i.e. for constructions that should be easy to assemble and afterwards take apart and move location. In such cases containers save time and money and substantially simplify transportation. However, there are cases where the use of other construction systems and materials might be more appropriate.

TEMPORALITY: A temporary restaurant on Seguin Island in Paris is bulit entirely from elements of temporary architecture (scaffolding, containers) yet has achieved a lasting image as high-quality architecture (by 1024 architecture).

Photo: Brice Pelleschi

Freitag video

CONTEXTUALITY:
Freitag specialize
in recycling
elements from
the transport
chain: they sell
bags and other
accessories made
from tarps and
for their shop in
Zurich they re-
cycled 19 freight
containers
(by Spillmann
Echsle).

Photo:Freitag.ch

TRANSFORMATION

Transforming containers into habitable spaces is not a demanding task, which is why people often do it themselves. The first step after selecting a container is to disinfect it. Afterwards a circular saw can be used to cut openings in the walls or remove redundant wall partitions. After painting, the container will be loaded, transported, and delivered on-site for assembly. Windows and doors will be fitted, followed by the roof and patios if planned. With smaller projects these transformation phases can be completed in a workshop, but generally take place on site, after assembly.

Once containers are put into place, they are screwed and welded together, and after the exterior rim of the construction is completed, work starts in the interior. First you need a subfloor and a sub-construction for ceilings and walls, which are often made of wood. The sub-construction will have insulation, electrical wiring, plumbing and other services built in. Walls and ceilings are usually finished in plaster, which makes the interior of a container home perfectly comparable with a traditional house. Plywood and OSB boards are also used, both as the final floor finish in budget projects as well as the sub-layer for the final floor finish (parquet, ceramics) in higher-end projects. The building is attached to power, plumbing and sewage infrastructure on site and furnished to the customer's taste.

Before transforming and delivering a container, however, it is necessary to lay the foundations. These depend on the weight of the construction and the ground's load bearing capacity: for major apartment buildings a concrete base is needed, while strip foundations and other types of foundations will often also work. If the ground is sufficiently firm, such as with event architecture set up in urban squares and car parks, extra foundations are not required.

Transformation of an empty metal box into a cosy single container apartment.
(c192 Nomad by HyBrid Architecture)

Recycled Shipping Container House, Sullivan County NY: the construction process in 11 steps.

Bigprototype.com

1. selecting appropriate containers

2. cutting out openings

3. painting the containers

4. transport to location

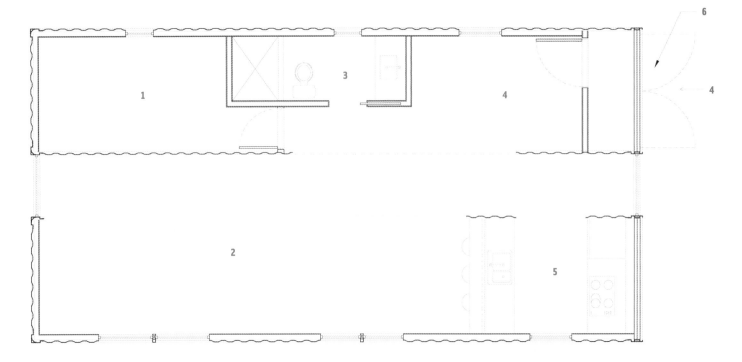

FLOOR PLAN

1. BEDROOM
2. LIVING-ROOM
3. BATH
4. ENTRY
5. KITCHEN
6. EXISTING CONTAINER DOORS

5. Site preparation / concrete foundations

6. placement on foundations

7. assembly on site

The Sullivan County Container House is a good example of how well container constructions adapt to demanding terrain. By Bigprototype (John Nafziger & Sarah Strauss) and Tim Steele Design.

11. final result

8. welding containers into place

9. roof construction

10. installing windows

Sturdy and durable

Shipping containers are ideal for building in many ways. They are designed to carry heavy loads and to be stacked high, and their frame structure is therefore very strong. They are designed to resist high winds and waves on ocean-going vessels, or road salt: they are therefore weather-resistant. They are practically unbreakable and have a long life-span.

Modularity

All shipping containers are made to standard measurements and as such they provide modular elements that can easily be combined into larger structures. This simplifies design, planning and transport.

Easy to transport

Containers are intermodal, which means they comply with stringent ISO standards regarding size, weight and capacity. This makes them perfectly compatible with all kinds of transport, such as ship, truck or rail, so they can be loaded onto as well as unloaded from the various segments of the transport chain easily and efficiently.

Lightweight

Container-based buildings weigh less than stone or concrete structures, which makes them safer in earthquake zones and requires less groundwork.

Availability

Used shipping containers are available or can be delivered anywhere around the world.

Cost

Used containers are available at a relatively low cost, especially compared to buildings constructed with labour-intensive methods. Costs are additionally driven down due to less groundwork required. Used shipping containers, which require simple modifications for conversion into housing/office units, can be purchased from major transport companies for as little as 1,200$ each. Brand new ones seldom cost more than 6,000$.

Sustainability

Containers are recyclable and reusable. Also, if buildings are constructed from containers, the use of other construction materials can be significantly reduced. All this makes container architecture comply with the 3R design concept: reuse, recycle, reduce.

Trendy

Container architecture that uses old shipping containers has been receiving a lot of encouraging attention from the world of design as well as the media for being a trendy green alternative to conventional buildings.

Temperature

Steel compounds overheat easily; container buildings will normally require better insulation than most brick, concrete or wooden structures. Untreated metal wrap on containers absorbs heat, but treated with the proper blend of non-toxic ceramic spheres or protected with a ventilated secondary roof the overheating can be prevented.

Waste

Transforming shipping containers into home/office units requires modifications, which results in waste.

Limited space

A single container makes for a very awkward living/working space, especially after it has been additionally insulated: it is a long narrow box of less than 2.4 m (8 feet) in height. To create spaces suitable for living and working, several containers need to be put together. Since they are meant for simple stacking one on top of the other, this can limit the architectural expression.

Manipulation

As opposed to the conventional construction materials, such as brick, concrete block and lumber, containers are too big and too heavy to be manipulated manually. Aa crane or forklift are therefore required at the construction site.

Building permits

The use of steel for construction, while prevalent in industrial construction, is not widely used for residential structures. Obtaining building permits may be troublesome in some regions due to municipalities not having seen this application before.

Pesticide-treated floors

Some shipping containers have pesticide-treated floors (arsenic, chromium, copper), which is a health hazard for humans. Such floors need to be disposed of and replaced before habitable.

Cargo spillages

A container can carry a wide variety of cargo during its working life. Spillages or contamination may have occurred on the inside surfaces and may have to be cleaned before they can be used for human habitation. Ideally all internal surfaces should be blasted to bare metal, and re-painted with a non toxic paint system.

Prejudice

People often still consider container architecture as suited only for workers, third world countries and the homeless, and don't recognise their added value in architecture.

CASE
STUDIES

Pierre
Morency Architecte
Chalet
Du Chemin Brochu

location: **Beaulac-Garthby, Quebec, Canada**

use: **Single family home**

year of completion: **2006**

photography: **Normand Rajotte**

no. of containers: **3**

The dynamic composition of containers and timber makes this retreat cabin something between a spacecraft and a tree house – which is exactly what the architect's children wanted.

FIRST FLOOR

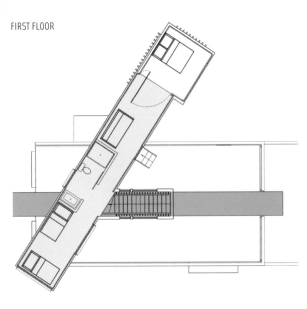

GROUND FLOOR

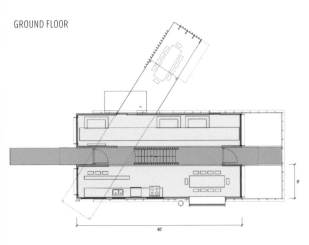

CELLAR

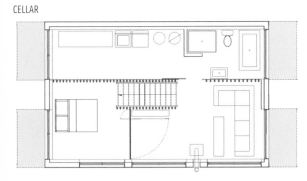

A stone's throw away from Lake Aylmer in Canada's Chaudière-Appalaches region, architect Pierre Morency set up a second home for his family. He paid tribute to the beautiful natural setting by preserving all trees on the site and by using nature-friendly construction materials. The main body of the house is three recycled shipping containers painted black, the interior of which is covered in recycled wood. The entire family participated in planning the building, and the children's wishes especially were taken very seriously; one of the sons wanted a spacecraft, another wanted a tree house. Their wishes came true. The top black container box floats away from its base, as if in space: the spacecraft. The entire house wears the coat of wooden panelling, the elevated first floor hovers among tree tops: a tree house.

The chalet has three layers. The exterior is covered in wooden panelling, underneath are the black recycled steel containers, while the interior has another wooden coating. Containers rest on a concrete base, which descends below ground level and hosts a guest suite and service room. The ground floor of the house consists of two containers set apart and a central wooden area connecting them, and accommodates the kitchen, dining room and living room. Further up is the third container, rotated to the side and supported by pillars. Here the atmosphere is more private, inside are the children's rooms, bath and master bedroom. The master bedroom lies in the wooden box stretching out of the container, offering breathtaking views of the lake. The containers' shorter sides are all glass and there are also many other windows, so that the house has plenty of daylight and the family enjoys a strong feeling of truly coexisting with the surrounding nature.

LOCATION

Adam Kalkin
12 Container House

location: **Brooklin, Maine, USA**

use: **Vacation Home**

year of completion: **2002**

photography: **Peter Aaron / Esto**

no. of containers: **12**

A gently sloping metal roof connects two orange six-container wings that are set apart to create a spectacular double-height fully-glazed living area in between them.

The 12 Container House is a custom-made prefabricated summer home, which architect Adam Kalkin created for the Adriance family from 12 recycled shipping containers. Kalkin designed a spacious residence with an extraordinary and even unusual appearance: it offers some 372 m2 (4,000 ft2) of interior surfaces and remains to this day probably the largest container residence ever. It is situated on a private plot outside the city of Brooklin in Maine, surrounded by trees and only steps from the sea shore. Constructed back in 2002 when private homes made from containers were still very rare, it attracted a lot of attention. It remains, however, one of the quintessential container architecture projects to this day.

Twelve orange containers are placed on a concrete base. Stacked into two levels they make two letters T, which are set at a distance to each other and have a large glazed area between them. This central two-level space lies at the heart of the symmetrical house and hosts a spacious living area, dining room and two staircases leading upstairs, each into its own T-winged part of the house. Containers on the ground floor house the kitchen, library, office, playground and guest bedroom. Because of the floor-to-ceiling windows and the glazed containers' shorter sides the house is very bright. The containers' glass sides in the interior allow good visual communication between the family members. The containers' longer sides function as the exterior wall on the outside but were fully removed on the inside in some parts (like the kitchen or the library) to make the interior more fluid and better connected to the central open space. The upstairs programme is more intimate, housing baths, bedrooms and office. The side of the house facing the sea has a large terrace with an outdoor fireplace.

GROUND FLOOR

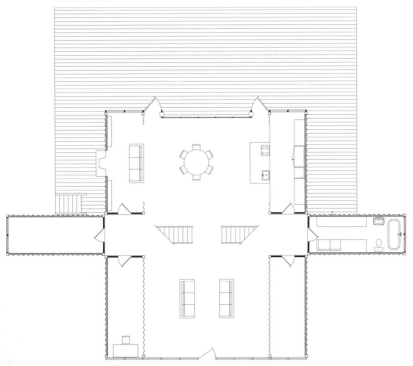

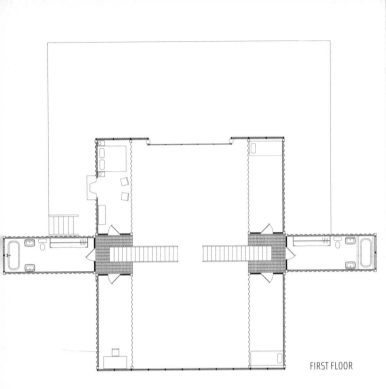

FIRST FLOOR

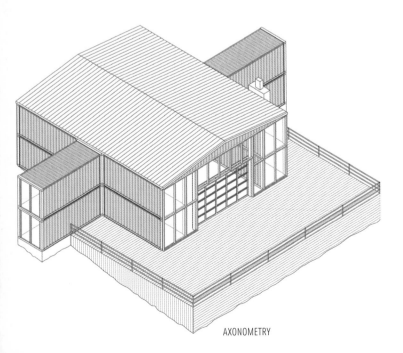

AXONOMETRY

FAÇADES

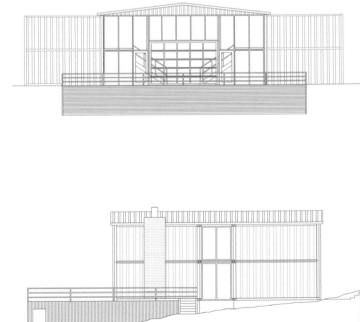

Stefan Beese
(Rebe Design)
Eco shipping
container lounge

location: **New Orleans, Louisiana, USA**

use: **Event Lounge**

year of completion: **2009**

photography: **Cat Wall, Stefan Beese, Mark Vinson, Melissa Bossola, Melissa Carrier, Melissa Shelton**

no. of containers: **6**

The signature event composition of containers, stacked into two levels and with event logo cut outs, takes the concert experience to a higher level.

Containers are very handy for staging temporary events, such as concerts, festivals, and fairs. They are quick to assemble on site and easy to relocate after use. They are especially convenient for artistic events because they can be arranged in a variety of inspiring constellations, creating diverse spaces inside and between each other.

When commissioned to construct a temporary grandstand and VIP lounge for the New Orleans Voodoo Music and Art Festival, Stefan Beese of REBE Design avoided traditional scaffolding and recycled six used 40' long shipping containers instead. The temporary structure not only housed a public grandstand and VIP lounge, but two bars with club seating and a remarkable elevated viewing platform near the main stage. The ground floor containers had large perforated cut outs spelling "Voodoo" which functioned as branding while also creating service area openings and affording further vistas. The unique and eco-friendly structure added to the distinctive setting of the New Orleans City Park, having endless design potential but little site impact.

After use, the recycled containers were disassembled and used as storage space for festival components. Eco Shipping Container Lounge was used again for the 2010 event, only this time the structure was improved with the addition of a 3 m (10') ADA lift leading up to the top deck. A similar layout was used for the 2011 festival and will continue to be used in the future as well as provide storage space during the year until each next installation. The Eco Shipping Container Lounge met all the design challenges put forth by the environment and the event itself, and even superseded expectations with its storage capacities and cost effectiveness. It will continue to be recycled for years to come.

Interview with Stefan Beese

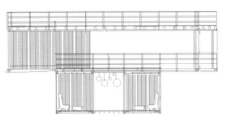

FAÇADES

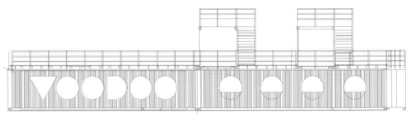

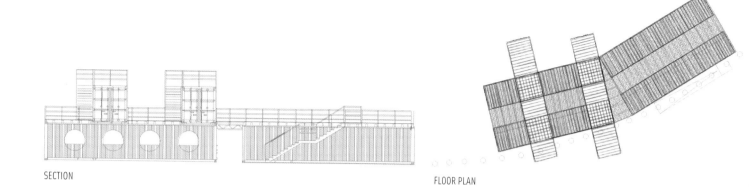

SECTION

FLOOR PLAN

Group 8
Cargo

location: **Geneva, Switzerland**

use: **Office Building**

year of completion: **2010**

photography: **Régis Golay, Federal Studio, Geneva**

no. of containers: **16**

Colourful and rugged containers, taken out of the transport chain as-they-were, stand out in stark contrast to the white minimalistic office environment. As opposed to the overall open landscape of the interior, containers congest specific programmes and services.

When moving to larger premises, Swiss-based architects group8 found a perfect location in a former industrial hall close to downtown Geneva. To make the best use of the 780 m2 (8,400 ft2) hall with ceilings 9 m (29.5') high, group8 arranged the interior into two zones: a spacious central space composed of informal meeting spaces for group work, and a two-level gallery along the rims of the hall constructed from 16 recycled shipping containers, which house various specific programmes.

The central common areas are bright and minimalistic, and give shape to a neutral environment, necessary for creative work. They constitute informal working spaces where employees can gather for group work, generating a strong exchange of ideas and powerful work flow. In this impeccable environment, the radiant containers symbolise the firm's global orientation. Into the white open space they bring a colourful cosmopolitan feel that was imprinted into them during their travels over the world's seas. They communicate with the staff and stimulate creative thinking.

This stark contrast between the overall white interior on the one hand and colourful containers dotted inside the hall on the other is Cargo's signature design feature. Containers were preserved "as found", i.e. without any outside cosmetic transformation, and look like they have been washed ashore directly out of the transport chain. The stark white background makes them stand out and catch your eye, which is in line with their function: as opposed to the more general function of the open space offices, containers accommodate specific and more private programmes such as relaxation rooms, model workshop, conference room, brainstorming room, eating lounge, and waiting room, which serve the entire hall. Colourful and rugged containers stacked against the perfectly white background fill the interior with a lively rhythm and create an inner skyline, a kind of miniature landscape, far away from traditional rigid office environments.

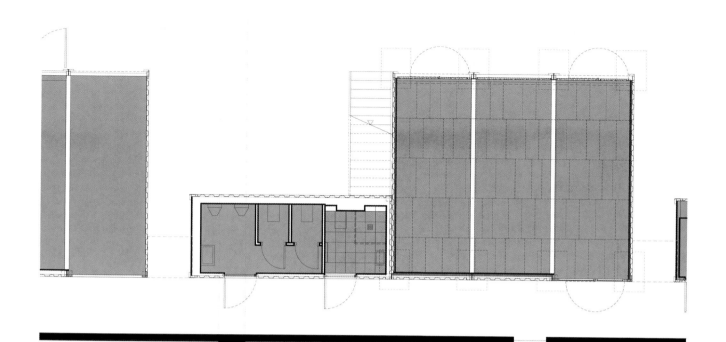

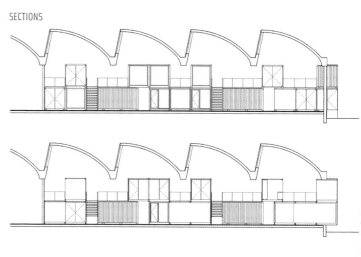

SECTIONS

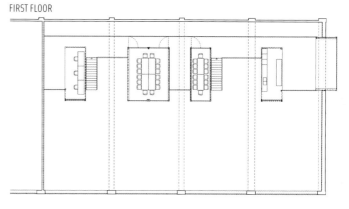

FIRST FLOOR

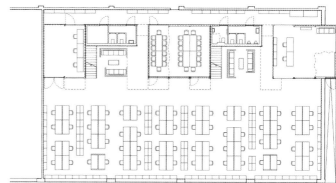

GROUND FLOOR

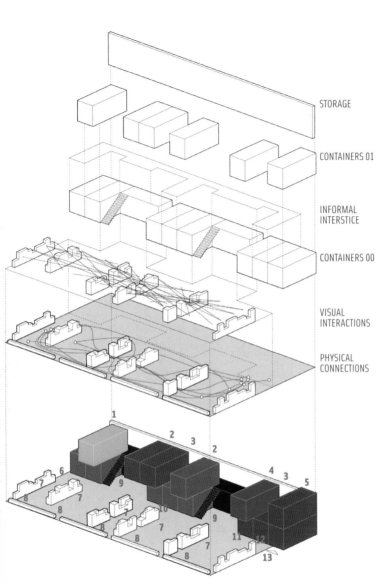

STORAGE

CONTAINERS 01

INFORMAL
INTERSTICE

CONTAINERS 00

VISUAL
INTERACTIONS

PHYSICAL
CONNECTIONS

1. BRAINSTORM
2. MEET
3. INFORMAL SPACE
4. EAT
5. RELAX
6. MODEL WORKSHOP
7. TEAM WORK
8. INFORMAL MEET
9. INFORMAL MEET RELAX
10. MEET / VIDEO CONFERENCE
11. INFO
12. WAIT
13. ACCESS

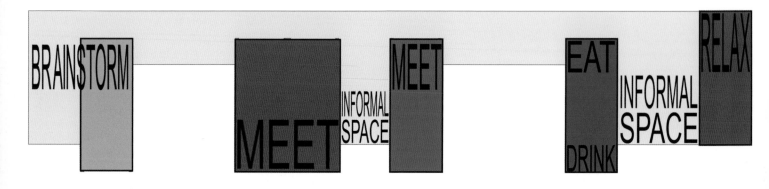

Yasutaka Yoshimura Architects
Bayside Marina Hotel

location : **Yokohama, Japan**

use: **Hotel Units**

year of completion: **2009**

photography: **Yasutaka Yoshimura**

no. of containers: **62**

Located between the marina and nearby park, and arranged into a dynamic composition, two-level hotel units faithfully follow the traditional Japanese design aesthetics.

Bayside Marina Hotel is a seaside cottage hotel. It differs from the other container projects in this book in two ways. First, it is not a single structure made from containers, but rather a series of independent pavilions creating a dynamic landscape composition.Secondly, it is not made from containers at all, but rather from modular units the size of standard 40'shipping containers.

The complex consists of 31 single-unit (flat) and double-height (maisonette) apartments, restaurant, entrance and services areas, all in the same modular system. Each unit is aligned differently, allowing ocean views of yachts moored at the adjacent marina as well as vistas of the nearby park. The physical separation of units enables for adequate sound insulation and more privacy, as well as creates a dynamic landscape. The sparing use of materials, exquisite details, gentle colour schemes and minimalist interiors as well as exteriors testify to the Japanese design. According to traditional Japanese aesthetics and the Tao ideal of emptiness, which sees a room's true beauty in the empty space between the roof and walls, interiors are furnished moderately and are not ruled by objects. The "container's" shorter sides are fully glazed, making the interiors very bright.

The prefabricated units were built in Thailand and then transported to Japan. By using not only the standard container dimension, but also the same locking hardware, the units were designed to be transported directly by a container ship. Assembly and finishing of the units was carried out in Thailand while the site in Japan was prepared in advance. After arrival on site, the units were simply bolted into place and connected to utilities, allowing for quick and economical on-site set up.

FIRST FLOOR

GROUND FLOOR

SECTION

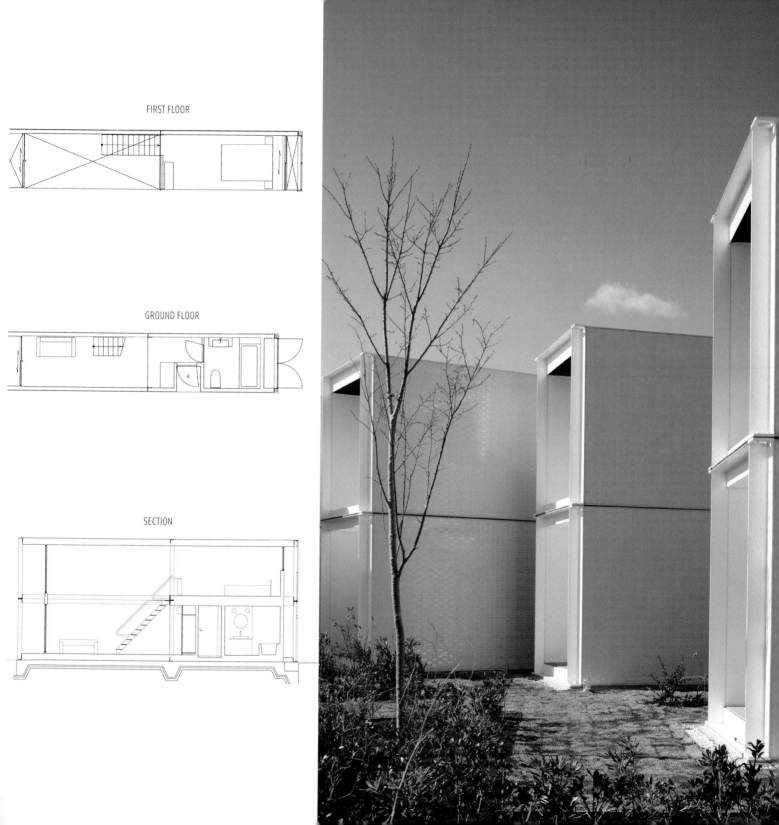

LOT-EK, Ada Tolla + Giuseppe Lignano
Puma City

location: **Ports around the world**

use: **shop, bar, lounge**

year of completion: **2008**

photography: **Danny Bright**

no. of containers: **24**

A branding promotion masterpiece, this mobile retail and event building consists of three levels of containers, shifted aside to create dynamic outdoor spaces, large overhangs and terraces.

Puma City is a transportable retail and event building that travels around the world. It consists of 24 containers and takes full advantage of the global shipping network already in place. The building is fully dismountable and travels on a cargo ship along with the sail boats; it will be assembled and disassembled a number of times once it reaches the different international harbours. Puma City is the first container building of its scale to be truly mobile.

The building is conceived as a three-level stack of containers, shifted to create internal outdoor spaces, large overhangs and terraces. It consists of two full retail spaces on the lower levels, both with large double heights as well as with 4-container-wide open spaces to challenge the modular box-quality of the container inner space; offices, press area and storage occupy the second level and a bar, lounge and event space with a large open terrace is at the top.

Puma City is also one of the largest ever brand promotion projects. The entire 24-container stack is coated in a facade with a strong graphic composition: it is branded with the super-graphic logo of the company, which is fragmented as a result of the stack shift. The fragmentation has nevertheless left the logo perfectly recognisable and has even built up its identity.

Puma City is designed to respond to all of the architectural challenges of a building of its kind, including the international building code, dramatic climate changes, plug-in electrical and HVAC systems and ease of assembly and operations. The building uses 40' shipping containers as well as a number of the existing container connectors to join and secure containers both horizontally and vertically. Each module is designed to ship as a conventional cargo container through a system of structural covering panels that fully seals all of its large openings for transport, and is removed on site when re-connecting the large, open interior spaces.

Puma City construction

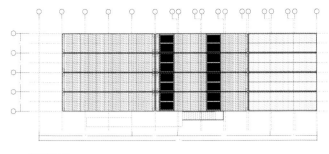

ROOF PLAN

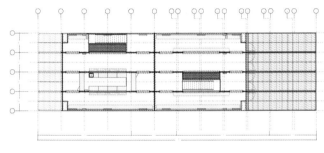

3rd FLOOR PLAN

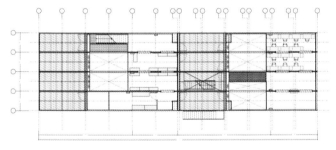

2nd FLOOR PLAN

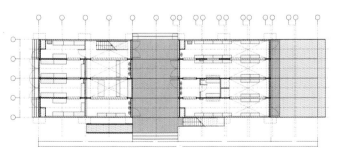

GROUND FLOOR PLAN

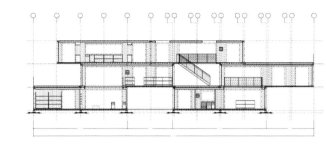

TYPICAL LONGITUDINAL SECTION

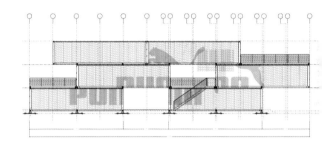

LONGITUDINAL ELEVATION

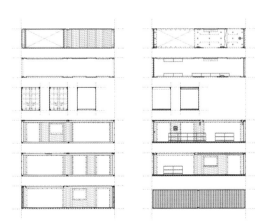

TYPICAL CONTAINER DRAWING

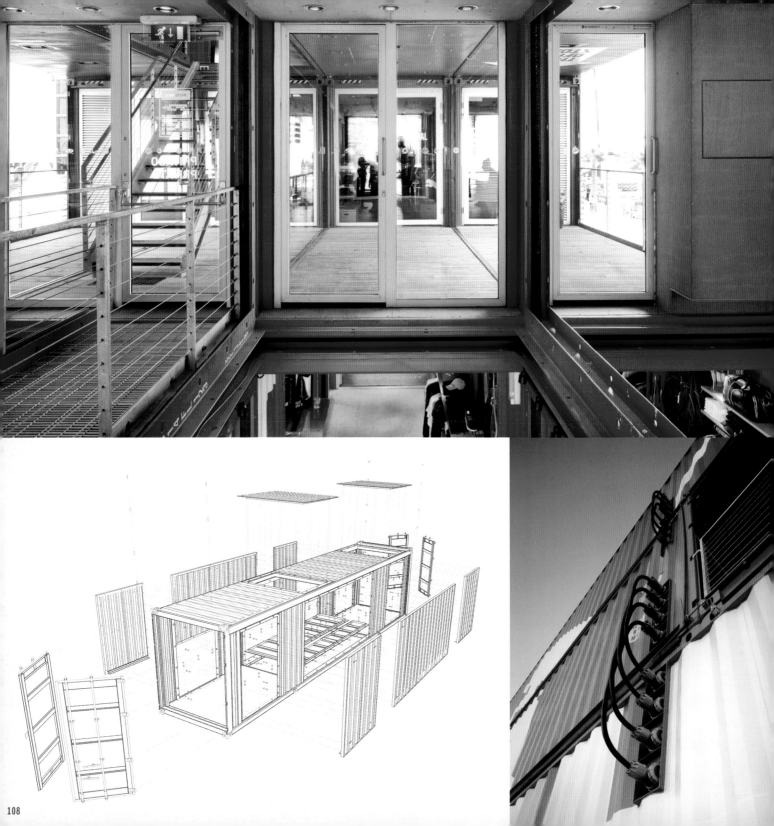

WALL COVER PANELS

ROOF COVER PANELS

FLOOR COVER PANELS

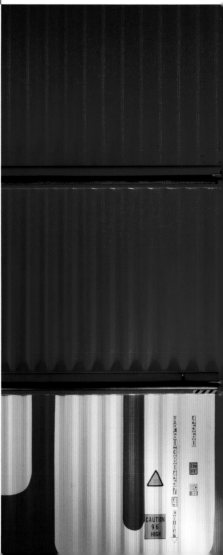

AXONOMETRY

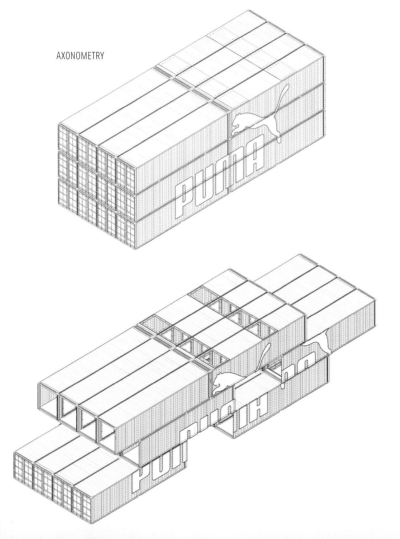

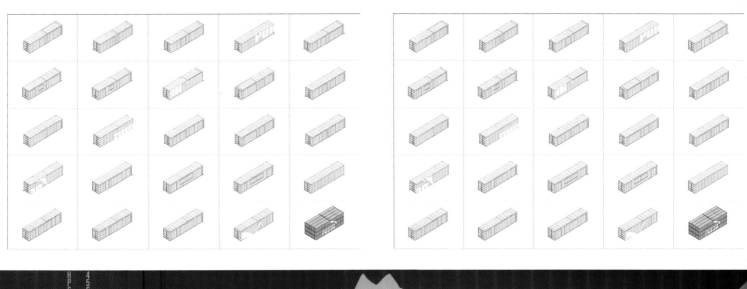

Studio MK27
Decameron

location: **São Paulo, Brasil**

use: **Showroom and office**

design team: **Marcio Kogan, Mariana Simas, Diana Radomysler**

year of completion: **2011**

photography: **Pedro Vannucchi**

no. of containers: **6**

The white opaque polycarbonate panels combined with vibrant containers create a trendy and spacious environment, perfect for a temporary design furniture shop in downtown São Paulo.

Brazil has significantly built up its profile on the global map in recent years, not merely in economic terms but in architecture as well. The retail furniture store Decameron in São Paolo is a small part of this story, offering a local design response to the building block of the culture of globalization.

The showroom of the Decameron furniture store is located on a rented site in the furniture commercial alley in São Paulo. To make the quick and economic construction viable, the project was based on the premise of a light occupation of the lot and done with industrial elements that are easy to assemble. The minimalist design combines an anonymous concrete element and translucent polycarbonate panels, and contrasts them with shipping containers in vibrant colours.

The fashionably stacked containers accommodate the furniture showroom. Two stories of containers, oriented perpendicular to the main street, form tunnels where products are displayed side by side. The concrete warehouse structure at the back of the plot houses the office. Separated from the showroom with a glass wall, designers in the office may overlook the activity in the store. The third design element is polycarbonate panels, which glow from the inside at night, showing shadows of people moving in the showroom. At the back of the lot there is a patio filled with trees and a pebbled-ground. When both doors are simultaneously opened, the whole store becomes integrated with its urban context, while at rush stressful hours, by opening only the back doors the store becomes self-absorbed, ruled by the presence of the inner-garden. At the same time Decameron is one with the intensity of urban life as well as a small nature retreat.

DECAMERON

droog

SECTIONS

Wardell+Sagan projekt
Wardell / Sagan residence

location: **San Francisco, California, USA**

use: **Office, guest room**

collaborators: **Pat Carson Studio, David Battenfield, David Strandberg**

year of completion: **2008**

photography: **Drew Kelly**

no. of containers: **2**

In the middle of their spacious loft slash art gallery, a San Franciso couple installed the biggest art piece of all: a composition of two reused shipping containers. The sculpture houses a guest bedroom with bath, and a home office.

Back in 2007 Jeff Wardell and Claudia Sagan had found a new home in the former Chinese laundry and tooth-powder factory with column-free interiors. The loft covers 266 m2 (2,860 ft2) and lies on a north–south axis with large windows at either end. To showcase their large art collection and maximize daylight, they decided to keep the entire large space open, apart from the master bedroom which they positioned at the back. Being passionate art lovers and collectors, Jeff and Claudia thought the huge double-height loft perfect for a home gallery. High ceilings and large wall surfaces allowed them to display even large-scale street art pieces, and eventually encouraged them to install into their apartment the largest art piece of all: a two-level sculpture composed of two containers close to perpendicular to each other.

The containers were hand picked in the Port of Oakland and seem a natural choice for the art and travel enthusiasts Jeff and Claudia. Being true cosmopolitans who have travelled the world over, it seems perfectly fitting they should furnish their home with formerly globetrotting shipping boxes. The two containers are joined with steel tubes and lashed to reinforced floor joints to make them earthquake-safe in the California's lower Pacific Heights. The bottom orange container accommodates a guest room with a custom Murphy bed and bath. The fully glazed guest bath wall is in fact a liquid crystal "privacy wall", which changes from clear to opaque at the flick of a switch. The upper blue container is a home office with a napping nook. Entry to the office is off a staircase leading up to the roof, where the family has a wellness area.

Dwell.com apartment presentation

ROOFTOP TERRACE

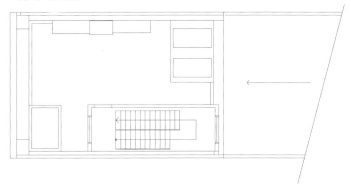

SECOND FLOOR

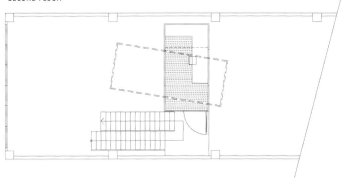

FIRST FLOOR

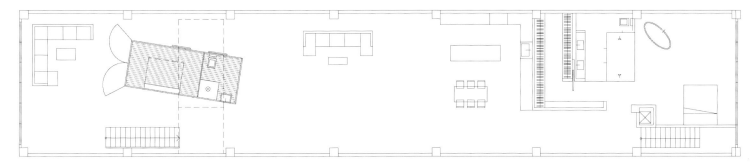

LOT-EK
Openschool

location: **Anyang, South Korea**

use: **Art school**

year of completion: **2010**

photography: **Sergio Pirrone, Kim Myung-Sik**

no. of containers: **8**

This container art piece slash art school completely denies the basic characteristics of container frames and sends the message that systems are to be changed here no matter how good they might be.

This conspicuous black-and-yellow art school stimulates creative thinking and inspires students by being an art piece in itself. The pointy container structure tells them that to create something awesome you do not need to start from scratch – sometimes you can take something and reuse it in a different, funky way. Due to its strong graphic image, OpenSchool is visible to cars and passersby alike, and serves as a landmark within the urban fabric of Anyang.

Eight angled converted shipping containers are sliced apart and randomly assembled back together to create a large arrow-like volume that hovers three meters over the landscape. The bold composition takes away containers' quintessential characteristic, structural self-sufficiency, and instead hoists container pieces up on black poles. This sends a strong message to young artists, encouraging them to think beyond established systems no matter how good they seem. The ground level footprint of the shipping container structure takes advantage of the existing sloping topography and serves as a public amphitheatre intended for public gatherings and community exchange.

The inside program includes one large, open, multi-purpose area that functions as a meeting/assembly room and exhibition space, as well as two studios for artists-in-residence. The two frontal walls, along the north-west axis and at the most dramatic overhang of the structure, are solid and pierced only by a series of peep-holes/tubes. Located at different heights to be accessible for kids and adults, they frame different views of the surrounding landscape, focusing on natural and urban moments of the neighbourhood. The short sides of the containers are entirely glazed to allow natural light, cross-ventilation and views toward the park path below.

A long, decked area at the third level stretches over the Anyang River. Resembling a diving-board, the roof deck offers an amazing view from its suspended position, while two long benches provide a place for social interaction.

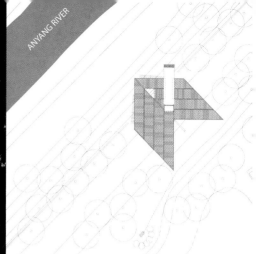

ANYANG RIVER

LOCATION

PLAN

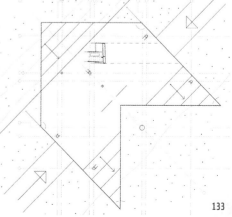

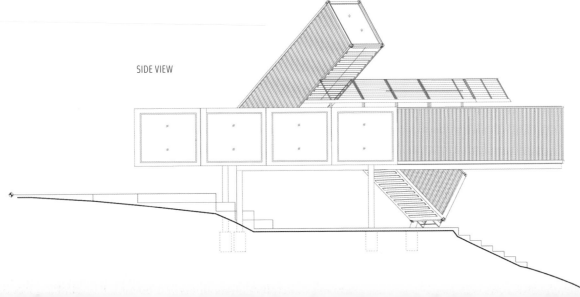

SIDE VIEW

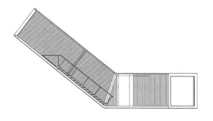

CONTAINER PARTS

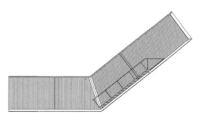

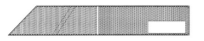

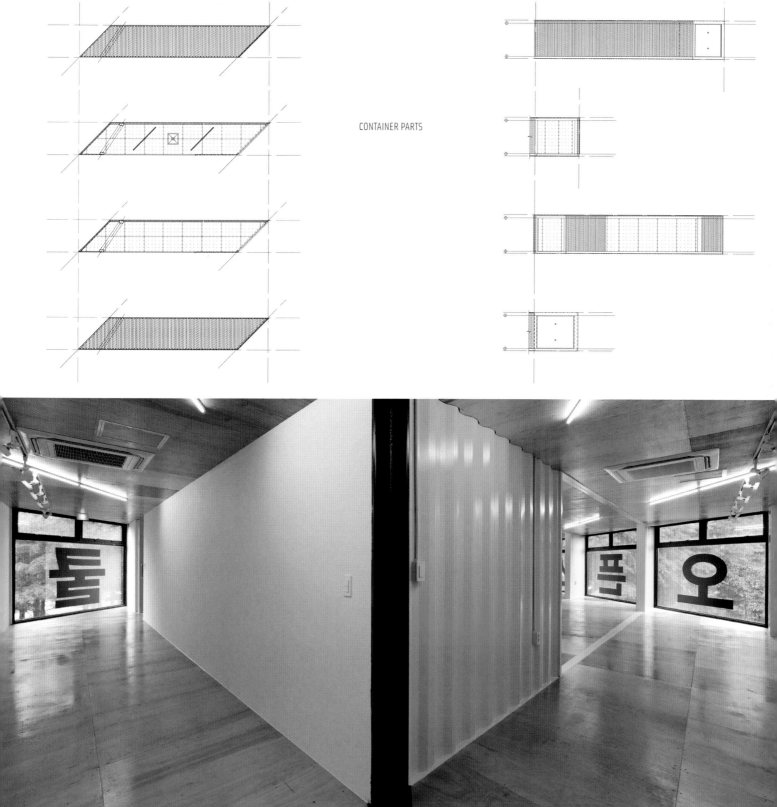

CONTAINER PARTS

Scabal (S Cullinan and Buck architects ltd)
Dunraven sports hall

location: **London, UK**

use: **Sports hall**

year of completion: **2009**

photography: **Jun Keung Cheung**

no. of containers: **30**

SCABAL have linked speed of construction with aesthetic appeal, low cost and sustainability to create an amazing multi-use sports hall.

The school wanted a sports hall that would be an amazing celebration of the school and their ambition, while the local authorities wanted one that fit within a rather slim budget. SCABAL took several months to marry these two things together: connecting speed of construction, aesthetic appeal, low cost and sustainability they managed to create an amazing multi use sports hall.

Sea containers have been used both as structure and internal accommodation to create an extremely simple and cost effective building that captures the participatory excitement of sports. Containers at each corner of the hall are painted into four primary colours so as to make the structure appear as if in fact created by four smaller buildings pushed together. The hall's industrial look is subtly undermined by the large window openings formed like giant greenhouses. The idea was to establish a connection between the industrial aesthetic of the hall and its suburban environment.

The image of back gardens is further supplemented by window stickers in the shape of watering cans and flowers, while the motif stretches further into the interior where cut outs in the shape of the trowel and the wheelbarrow function as a viewing gallery.

The clear glazing and the arrangement of the 'greenhouses' as well as the internal openings in the galleries all allow the interior to be flooded with natural daylight. This also makes the space suitable for exams, assemblies and other events. The glazing allows glimpses of activity within the hall from the outside, connecting the building with its environment – something too often lacking in the brick box sports halls. At night, when the hall becomes available for community use as a sports facility or a multi-purpose hall, this composition of openings makes the street frontage of the building glow while the lit-up window shapes around the sides further animate the form.

Project video

SIDE FAÇADE

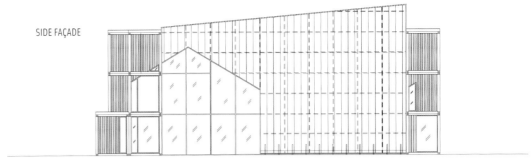

FRONT FAÇADE

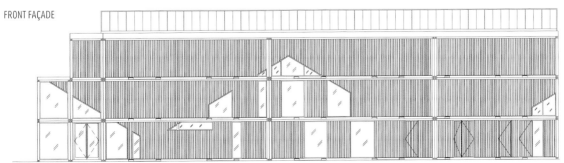

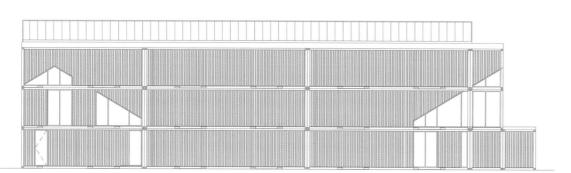

BACK FAÇADE

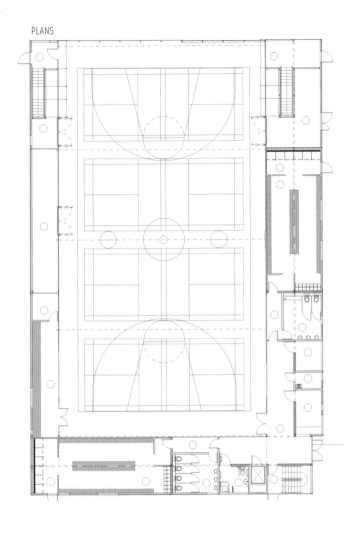
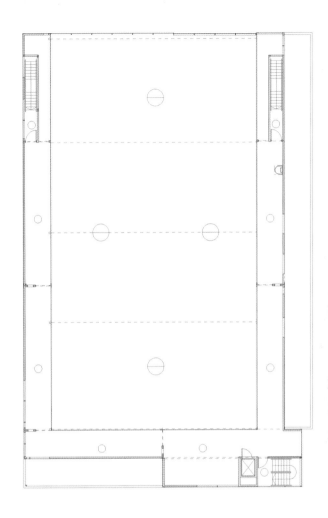
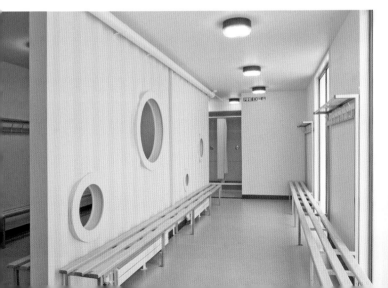

We Like Today
Boxpark

location: **Londres, UK**

use: **Centre Pop up**

year of completion: **2011**

photography: **Guy Archard, Boxpark**

no. of containers: **72**

BOXPARK is a good example of how even temporary buildings can help upgrade abandoned strips of land, bringing to the community a live gallery of 60 shops that are all inside containers but very diverse in design.

Most traditional retail developments try to sign their tenants up to five- and 10-year leases. In the current economic environment, this is a real liability. In BOXPARK, Roger Wade leases containers for as little as one year. BOXPARK is a retail revolution – the world's first pop-up mall – and only the first in an ambitious series of temporary eco-friendly pop-up shopping malls offering a carefully selected array of brands.

BOXPARK consists of 60 standard-size shipping containers, stripped and refitted to create unique, low cost, low risk, 'box shops'. They are stacked two stories high and five rows wide. Each container is leased out to selected brands, creating a vibrating community of over 40 retailers, cafes, restaurants and galleries. BOXPARK is located on a vacant strip of east London's fashionable Shoreditch High Street that has been empty for 40 years, but the great thing is that it can move easily. If one of the shops feel they are not getting the most out of the current location, the idea is they can potentially move to another part of the country without having to close down or dismantle a thing.

BOXPARK represents a convenient alliance of economy and ecology, providing a cheap exciting retail space without extensive plundering of resources: the containers and supporting structures were assembled on-site in a matter of weeks, saving on costs and waste. The box walls are thickly insulated, making heating more efficient and eliminating the need for air conditioning. When their lease term is up, the entire BOXPARK can be disassembled and recycled for future use, and the land be given back to its owners in exactly the same condition as before.

Boxpark Video

GROUND FLOOR

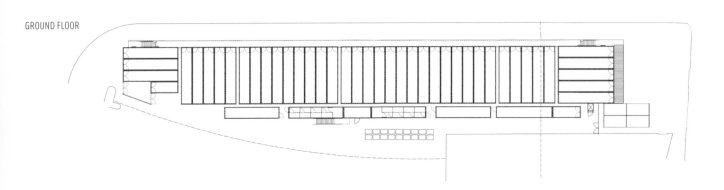

FIRST FLOOR

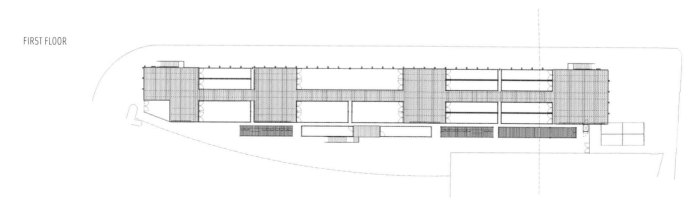

Phooey Architects
Children`s activity centre

location: **Melbourne, Australia**

use: **Activity center**

year of completion: **2009**

photography: **Peter Bennetts**

nr. of containers: **4**

The four containers – along with the staircases, projecting roofs and large wooden terrace – have been arranged so as to give the impression of a stranded pirate ship in an amusement park, which the children no doubt appreciate.

Although some container structures try to beautify containers or even conceal them so as to make the buildings appear more conformist, Melbourne's Children`s Activity Centre by Phooey Architects goes back to the basics. Rusty patches and logos of shipping carriers on the facade remain clearly visible and are interrupted only by an occasional window opening. The four containers – along with the staircases, projecting roofs and large wooden terrace – have been arranged so as to give the impression of a stranded pirate ship in an amusement park, which the children no doubt appreciate. The little users of the pirate ship therefore feel perfectly at home there, also due to its composition, since they are very much inclined to recycle and make innovative use of available materials themselves (this is especially evident when they construct hiding places using every possible item close to hand).

Two larger containers sit on the ground and support the two smaller ones, rotated by 45 and thus overhanging the bottom structure. A large part of the bottom two containers' roofs is left bare to form the "ship's deck" – a spacious wooden terrace, which is connected to the ground by an external staircase. The staircase boasts an original decorum made of container steel leftovers from cuts for window and door openings. The fence and projecting roof on the first floor are of the same making. The balconies wedged between the two door wings of standard containers provide shade in summer, while winter comfort is achieved through orientation and ample insulation.

The interior is simple, with the largest space being the so-called flexible multiuse room on the ground floor. Lined with chequered carpet tiles, it is used for study, painting, dancing and lounging about. The "ship" is surrounded by trees, garden, pond and assortment of sandpits and play areas, which further creates a genuine adventure playground.

FIRST FLOOR

GROUND FLOOR

MMW of Norway
GAD

location: **Oslo, Norway**

use: **GAllery**

year of completion: **2005**

photography: **Erik Førde**

nr. of containers: **10**

The dynamic, Jenga-game-like composition of containers hosts three galleries over three floors, in addition to an open air roof top exhibition terrace.

GAD is a mobile gallery for contemporary art consisting of ten steel shipping containers, currently located in an inner city park in Oslo. The owner, Alexandra Dyvi, wanted a semi temporary gallery, so containers came as a first and best choice. The three-level construction is easy to assemble or take apart, so it can be transported and set up at another location within a matter of days.

GAD used to stand all alone at the tip of the pier at Tjuvholmen overlooking the Oslo fjord. To pay tribute to traditional shipbuilding craftwork, MMW created the gallery using shapes that remind us of ships, such as the circular windows placed opposite each other on the first floor. Industrial ladders/stairs and containers are another link with the shipbuilding and transport industry.

Containers are composed in the manner of the "Jenga" game. The largest exhibition room in the gallery is on the ground floor and consist of five 20` containers. These support the first floor, which includes three 40` containers combined in the shape of the letter U. Access to the gallery is on the first floor via an industrial exterior staircase. The first floor hosts the reception desk, service room, storage and a small gallery space that includes a staircase leading further up to the second floor gallery, composed of two containers. The interior is insulated and finished in plywood and drywall, the walls covered with artwork. The gallery is well illuminated, with magical northern daylight entering through glazed shorter container sides as well as round window openings. All these openings offer inspiring views of the surroundings and create an open, breezy feeling.

GAD 3D model

GROUND FLOOR PLAN

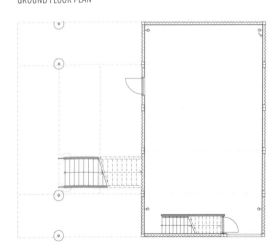

1ST FLOOR PLAN

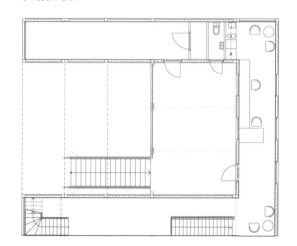

2nd FLOOR PLAN

SIDE FAÇADE

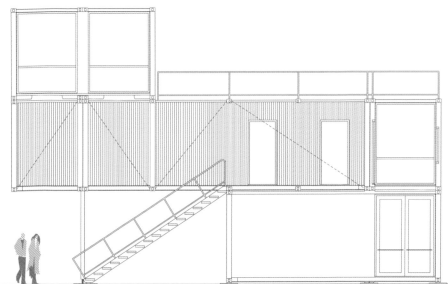

FRONT FAÇADE

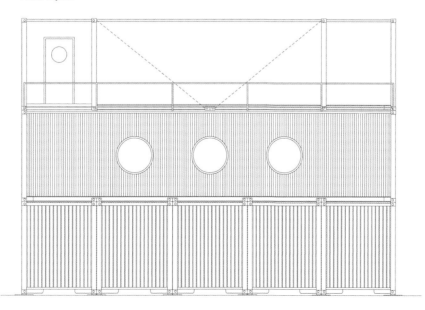

Christophe Nogry
House Extension

location: **Nantes, France**

use: **House Extension**

year of completion: **2009**

photography: **Stéphane Chalmeau**

no. of containers: **2**

The Nantes family home extension is a good example of how containers can help enhance living conditions speedily and effectively.

Two used navy blue shipping containers have found a new home in inland France. In suburban Nantes, in a neighbourhood from the 1960s, they have helped expand a family home that had become too tight for its tenants. Since the house's central position on the narrow plot left little space for an extension, three-and-a-half meter wide containers seemed perfect for the job.

Mounted one on top of the other, the containers attach to the house on its south side. The ground floor one (ISO 40') is twice the size of the upper floor one (ISO 20'). Standard container width barely suffices for a living space, therefore an intermediate buffer zone was inserted between the existing building and the container extension. The wooden skeleton was fitted with insulation and finished in concrete slabs, adding one meter of space along the entire length of the extension on both floors. The buffer zone has thus expanded the interior centrally, which is precisely where the existing house felt most crowded.

The larger, ground floor container accommodates a multimedia and relaxation room. With a floor-to-ceiling bookshelf the entire length of the container, TV and hi-fi system, it functions as an extension of the existing living room. The container's two smaller sides have window openings: to the north-west a small one facing the street, and to the south east a fully glazed side with a door that leads into the enclosed garden. The smaller, upper container houses a new master bedroom with a bathroom. The former bedroom was transformed into a spacious walk-in closet and now leads into the extension. The same as on the ground floor, the additional width between the house and its extension makes the interior on the upper floor more spacious and comfortable. Walls, ceilings and floors on both floors are finished in light gray wood-cement slabs, which together with lighting create a pleasant domestic atmosphere.

FIRST FLOOR PLAN

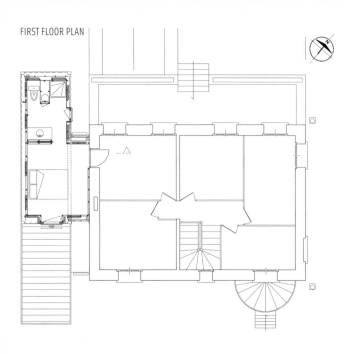

SECTION

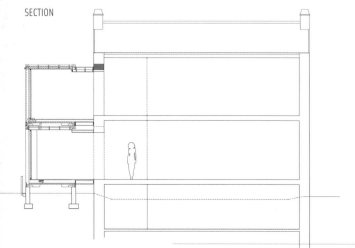

FAÇADES

Joe Haskett, Distill Studio
Box office

location: **Providence, Rhode Island, USA**

use: **office building**

year of completion: **2010**

photography: **Nat Rea, Glenn Turner, Stephanie Ewens**

no. of containers: **35**

Box Office is an example of ecologically responsible architecture offering cargo offices to people who don't mind thinking outside of the box from the inside of one.

Thinking inside of the box may become the newest trend for creative thinkers thanks to the 12-unit office and studio building called Box Office. Constructed from 32 repurposed shipping containers, the building in Providence, Rhode Island is a working haven for companies and individuals looking for a cheerful, comfortable and eco-friendly place to think. Distill Studio, now one of the tenants, designed Box Office as a high performance, low impact building consisting of spatially efficient units ranging in size from 60m2 (640 ft2) (a two-bay unit) to 149 m2 (1,600 ft2) (a five-bay unit) intended for small businesses, start-up entrepreneurs and incubator spaces.

The design for Box Office emerged after the economy degraded and the client needed a more budget-friendly solution. Besides using cost-effective recycled shipping containers, energy efficiency was a high priority. This included the use of high performance, non-petroleum insulation, doors and windows to minimize heat loss in and out of the office spaces. Numerous cut windows pull daylight into the interior, and a large canopy in the centre of the building protects the inner courtyard and shades the space in the summer. As a result of the designers' maxim "big ideas, small footprints", Box Office is 25–30% more energy efficient than the building code requires. Conceptually testifying to its origin, each container features a "truth window", which is where the container's label was left unpainted so everyone can see its serial number.

Sitting just off the railway track and New York–Boston highway route, the blue, green and yellow Box Office containers easily catch the attention of commuters. The building consists of two wings set slightly apart and connected by a roofed walkway. This makes it appear greater and lets the space between containers catch more air. To create a more dynamic design, a few containers were pulled out of the stack by one-third, creating a diverse interplay of cantilevered conference rooms and outdoor walkways and staircases.

Box office assembly

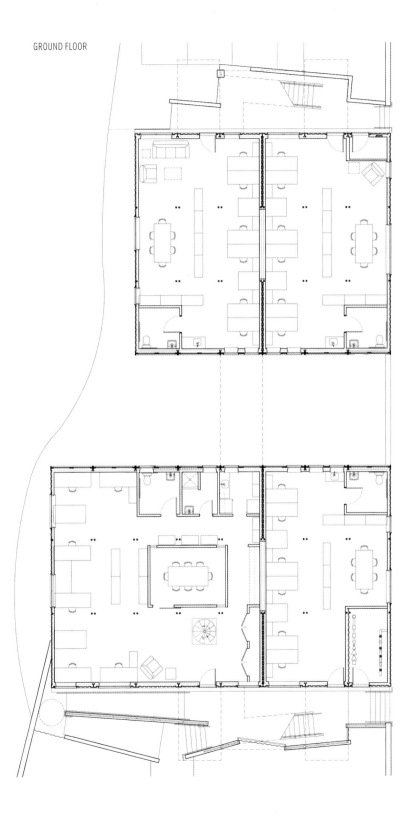

GROUND FLOOR

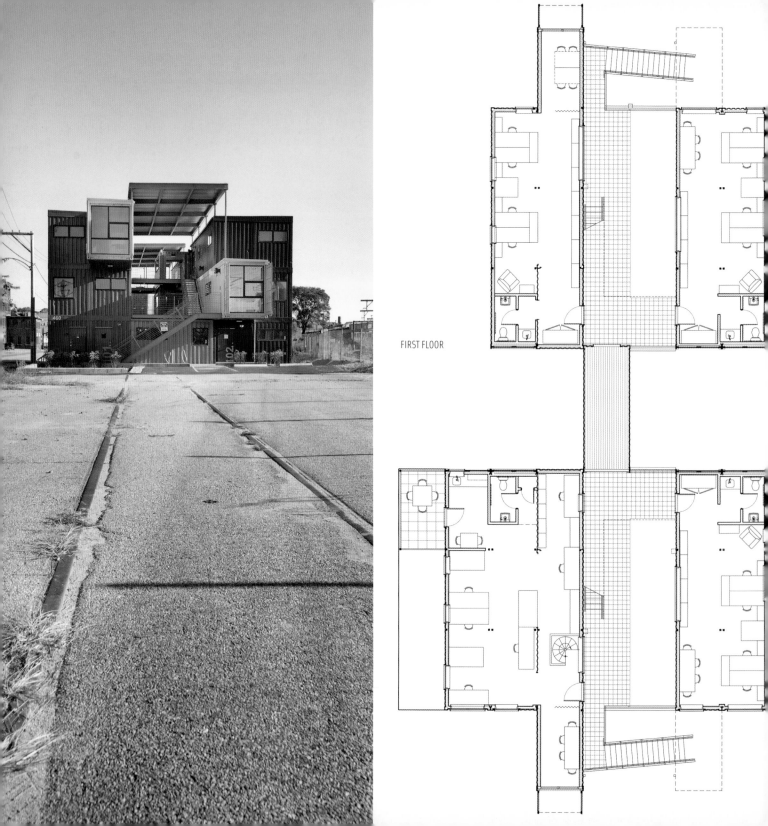

FIRST FLOOR

Ralph Webster, City of Melbourne
The Venny

location: **Melbourne, Australia**

use: **Childrens Center**

collaborators: **Stuart Nicoll, Paul Mckeogh, Aliey Ball, Dani Von Der Borch, John Rayner & Kirsten Raynor**

year of completion: **2010**

photography: **Andrew Wuttke, Ralph Webster**

no. of containers: **5**

This community building near the docks of the Port of Melbourne incorporates a wide series of ecological features to create an educational and joyous environment for the local children.

GROUND FLOOR

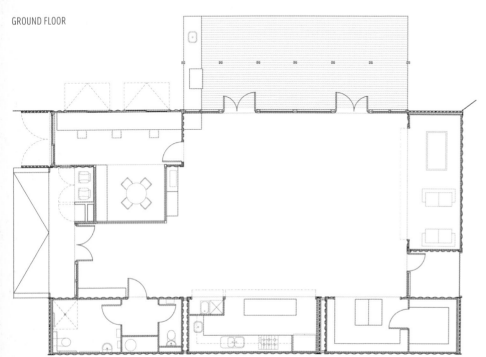

SUSTAINABLE PRINCIPLES
USED IN THE PROJECT INCLUDE:

- ORIENTATION

- SOLAR SHADING

- NATURAL DAY LIGHTING TO EVERY SPACE

- NATURAL VENTILATION

- RAINWATER HARVESTING

- VERY HIGH THERMAL INSULATION VALUES

- HIGH PERFORMANCE DOUBLE GLAZING

- THERMAL INERTIA – THERMAL MASS AND
  PHASE CHANGE PLASTERBOARD

- PASSIVE NIGHT PURGE COOLING

- SOLAR HOT WATER SYSTEM

- PHOTO-VOLTAIC PANELS – THE BUILDING
  PRODUCES MORE POWER THAN IT USES

- RECYCLED MATERIALS

- EXTENSIVE GREEN ROOF

The Venny is a free communal backyard and play space for children aged 5–16, located in an inner city park in Melbourne. It is constructed from five refurbished second-hand 20' shipping containers, which each serve a unique function: cooking, storage, office, lounge. They are arranged to form a U shape, creating a large free multi-purpose activity space in between. They can be closed with a roller door when not in use, which reduces the area that staff need to monitor and after hours along with the front entry roller door strengthens security. However, closed roller doors also eliminate the usual surfaces where children put up their drawings. The Venny has solved this problem in an unusual way: on the floor of the multipurpose room is a large art piece made from children's drawings and other art pieces. Over 100 children helped create the art piece, which is embedded in a layer of clear epoxy resin. The underlying philosophy for the design was to create a facility that is joyous and playful, whilst delivering a building that is highly functional, robust enough to handle a thousand children a week and an educational exemplar of sustainable design.

Starting with the extensive green roof, which protects bare containers from overheating as well as wear and tear, Venny's eco-friendly features were developed in cooperation with the University of Melbourne. Other features that help the building produce more power than it uses include use of recycled materials (starting with containers), optimum north-bound orientation to profit from the Australian sun, natural day lighting to every space, passive cooling, rainwater harvesting, high performance double glazing, photovoltaic panels, and so on and so on…

FAÇADES

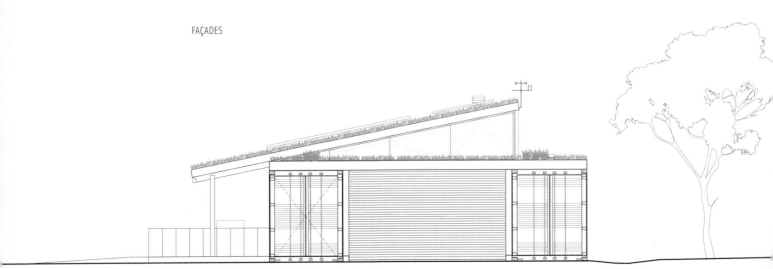

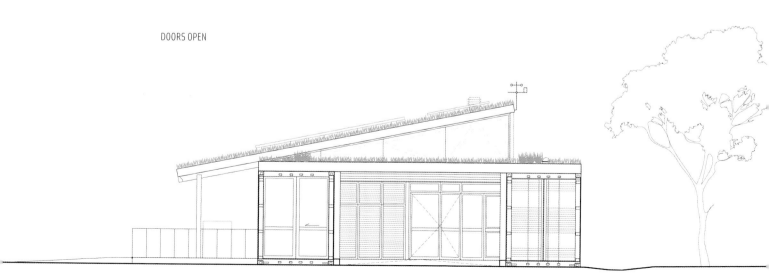

DOORS OPEN

SECTION

SOLAR TUBE
VENTURI VENTILATOR
SOLAR HOT WATER
PHASE CHANGE PLASTERBOARD
5.1 KW PHOTOVOLTAIC ARRAY

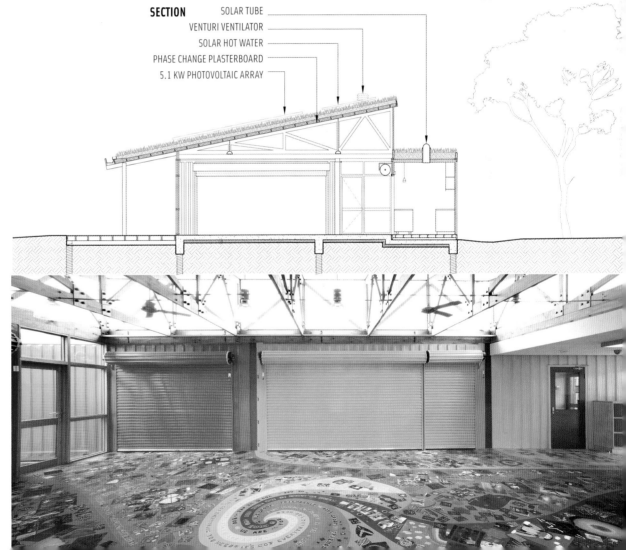

Arhitektura
Jure Kotnik
Kindergarten Ajda 2

location: **Ravne na Koroškem, Slovenia**

use: **Kindergarten**

collaborators: **Andrej Kotnik, Tjaša Mavrič, Tina Marn**

project year: **2011**

photography: **Miran Kambič**

no. of containers: **16**

The anthracite magnetic façade connects containers into a protective cluster. It functions as a convenient teaching tool, supports the learning process and – by constantly changing the kindergarten's appearance – triggers children's imagination day after day.

Kindergarten Ajda is the extension of a kindergarten in Ravne na Koroškem, a small town in northern Slovenia. It has replaced a former temporary kindergarten extension, which was set up from three containers and had one playroom, offering at the time immediate relief for lack of kindergarten space. To create a permanent extension, thirteen 20' ISO containers were added to the three existing ones and all of them carefully incorporated into a unique whole. Ajda's containers are arranged into clusters and joined by a single roof, with spaces in between used for various purposes such as dressing room, covered terraces and multi-purpose entrance.

Ajda consists of a total of 16 containers, which host three classrooms, two covered terraces and two washrooms for children, all of them dynamically connected with the dressing room and multi-purpose entrance hall. The interior is not only spacious but very bright, since the playrooms' longer walls are fully glazed to enable children good visual communication with the green surroundings. The spacious multi-purpose entrance hall functions as a gallery for children's artwork, play area and reading nook, and is equipped with a mobile theatre screen. One corner of the kindergarten was made into roofed open-air terraces in teak wood, allowing for the children to play outside well protected from weather inconveniences all year round.

The signature design feature of kindergarten Ajda is its didactic façade, made from thick anthracite isolative and fire-resistant boards covered in colourful magnets of five colours. The lightweight magnets are foldable so that children can manipulate them with ease, combining colourful design blocks to create animals, vehicles, buildings and other imaginary shapes. The interactive façade helps improve children's motor skills, eye-hand coordination and problem-solving techniques, as well as stimulates creativity and encourages the matching of colours, shapes and sizes.

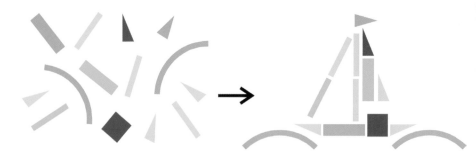

Kindergarten Ajda's magnetic facade:

1. Is a toy that allows children to arrange magnets into various shapes, such as animals, vehicles, buildings and imaginative designs;
2. Helps children develop problem-solving skills, creativity , sort relationships, as well as match colours, shapes and sizes;
3. Helps improve eye-hand coordination and motor coordination;
4. Enhances children's creativity and intelligence, their IQ and EQ;
5. Is a didactic tool for teachers and can support the learning process;
6. Is a design novelty that combines interest, benefit and creativity

Ajda Video

GROUND FLOOR

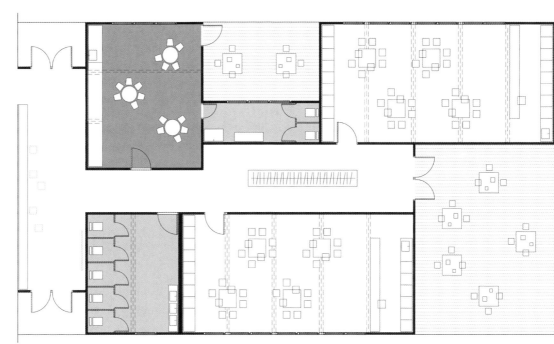

199

MAGNETS

SECTIONS

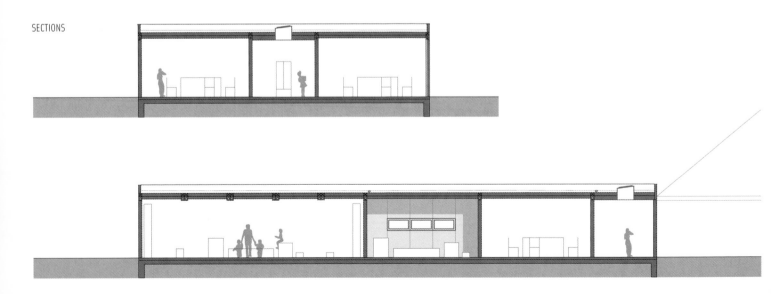

CONSTRUCTION PHASES

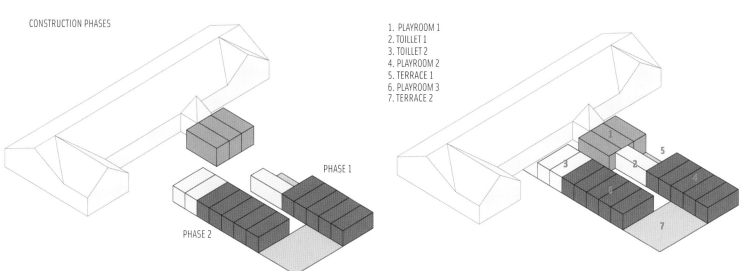

1. PLAYROOM 1
2. TOILLET 1
3. TOILLET 2
4. PLAYROOM 2
5. TERRACE 1
6. PLAYROOM 3
7. TERRACE 2

PHASE 1

PHASE 2

Platoon
Kunsthalle Gwangju

location: **Gwanju, South Korea**

use: **Cultural Centre**

year of completion: **2010**

photography: **Platoon**

no. of containers: **29**

Kunsthalle Gwangju is a hub city of Asian culture booming with numerous and diverse events. Platoon's winning recipe could well be imported back to Europe: in containers, of course.

Kunsthalle Gwanju is the second project by Berlin's Platoon Cultural Development team built in South Korea. Following the success of the first Kunsthalle in Seoul, Asia Munhwa Maru (its Korean name) is its younger brother, bringing a mix of Korean, Asian and global cultural performances to the city of Gwanju. It is a place where artist meet and interact with the visitors, creating and experiencing new cultural strategies of contemporary society. In addition to what one would expect to find in a cultural centre, like art exhibitions, concerts, dance and other art performances, Kunsthalle Gwanju also features movie nights, lectures, discussions and brainstorming sessions, fashion shows and flea markets.

Asia Munhwa Maru consists of 29 piled up containers stacked up three levels high creating a quadratic cube. The video screen on the 3rd floor can be seen from the outside and attracts passers-by, inviting them inside. The interior is designed as large open and flexible spaces, available for various purposes: multifunctional space, media wall, art library (with culture related publications), art lounge (place where people can meet and talk). The two-level hall is especially suitable for indoor concerts.

The interior design is neutral, mostly white, and serves as an unobtrusive background for various performances. Lighting is created separately for each of them, creating customised ambients. The first floor houses an art gallery and also functions as a balcony for bigger performances, while the ground floor hosts all the infrastructural programmes that service the entire Kunsthalle, like bar, kitchen, library and artists' room. On the outside there is an art yard of similar size as the indoor hall, bordered with two levels of containers, with storage facilities on the ground and balconies on the first level – a great place for concerts and other art related open air happenings, where people can meet and talk, act as artists and contribute to the programme or just observe as guests.

Platoon.org Video

ROOF

GROUND FLOOR
1. STORAGE
2. ARTIST ROOM
3. OFFICE
4. ART SHOP
5. LIBRARY
6. ART YARD BAR
7. ART LOUNGE BAR
8. KITCHEN
9. ENTRANCE

FIRST FLOOR
1. BALCONY
2. ART GALLERY
3. BRIDGE
4. ACCES EXHIBITION
5. ART DECK

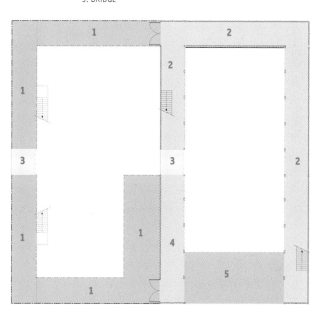

FRONT VIEW ENTRANCE

VIDEO FACADE

ENTRANCE

SIDE VIEW

ART YARD   MAIN HALL

Dpavilion Architects
Contertainer

location: **Batu, East Jawa, Indonesia**

use: **Health clinic, Library**

collaborators: **Edwin Nafarin, Khamawardhana**

Heksa Putera, Kartika Ciputera

year of completion: **2008**

photography: **Ganny Gozaly**

no. of containers: **5**

The health clinic offers free health care while the public library inside colourful reused containers widens people's horizons and paves the community's way past the society manufacturing commodities for the West into a knowledge society.

Contertainer is a health clinic and public library in Batu, East Jawa that repurposes containers to house a health clinic and a public library. The name is an amalgam of two words: container and entertainer, which reflects its goal of providing a better quality of living for those who have little money. All services inside this playful and colourful project are namely free to the public.

The center is composed of five shipping container hoisted up on top of stilts. The health clinic on the first floor is wrapped in a sterile white steel construction and stands in stark contrast with the library that spreads on the second and third floor in red, yellow, blue and light green containers th stick out in mid air. The bright colours symbolize the myriad of knowledge that books, which serve as "windows" to the world at large, bring to the people of Batu. Books educate and entertain ther as well as offering glances of the many different worlds and continents that containers might have travelled before they had docked in to become their public library. The third floor setting offers views of the city, the surrounding landscape and beyond. Shipping containers are easily accessible and cheap in Indonesia, and Dpavilion Architects decided to use them because of their multi-functional properties and ease of construction.

The colourful containers are positioned in differe directions and at irregular angles, breathing into the composition some of the dynamics of sea-faring. The bold scheme is complemented by supporting stilts of the same colours, which give the structure a daring edge.

There is a deeper philosophical side to the story as well. Indonesia used to be sweatshop hub providing goods to the West and goods are still shipped there in containers. In an attempt to stop the country from being a distributor of foreign products, some of these vessels have been retained as architectural pieces giving back to the society.

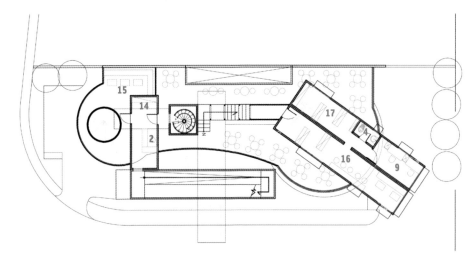

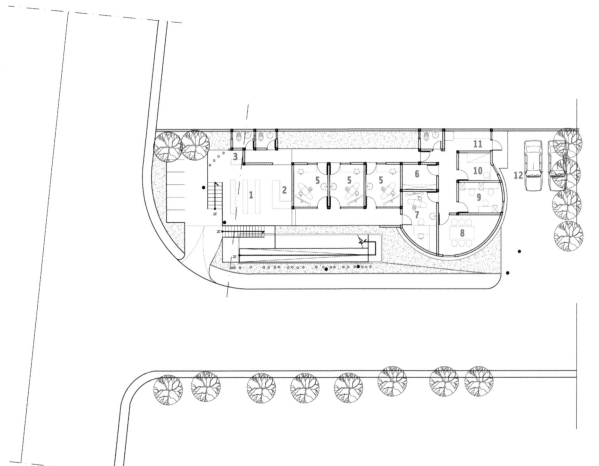

GROUND FLOOR PLAN

1. WAITING ROOM
2. RECEPTION
3. SECURITY
4. TOILET
5. DENTIST ROOM
6. POTION ROOM
7. RADIOLOGY
8. MEETING ROOM
9. BACK OFFICE
10. RESTROOM
11. PANTRY
12. CAR PARKING
13. MOTORCYCLE PARKING
14. LOCKER
15. OPEN SPACE
16. READING ROOM
17. COLLECTION ROOM

2ⁿᵈ FLOOR PLAN

16

16

FACADE

LOT-EK
Sanlitun South

location: **Beijing, China**

use: **Shopping Centre**

year of completion: **2008**

photography: **Shuhe Architectural photography**

no. of containers: **151**

Sanlitun South recreates the atmosphere of a traditional Beijing hutong and brilliantly brings to life the spirit of an ancient market place within contemporary architecture.

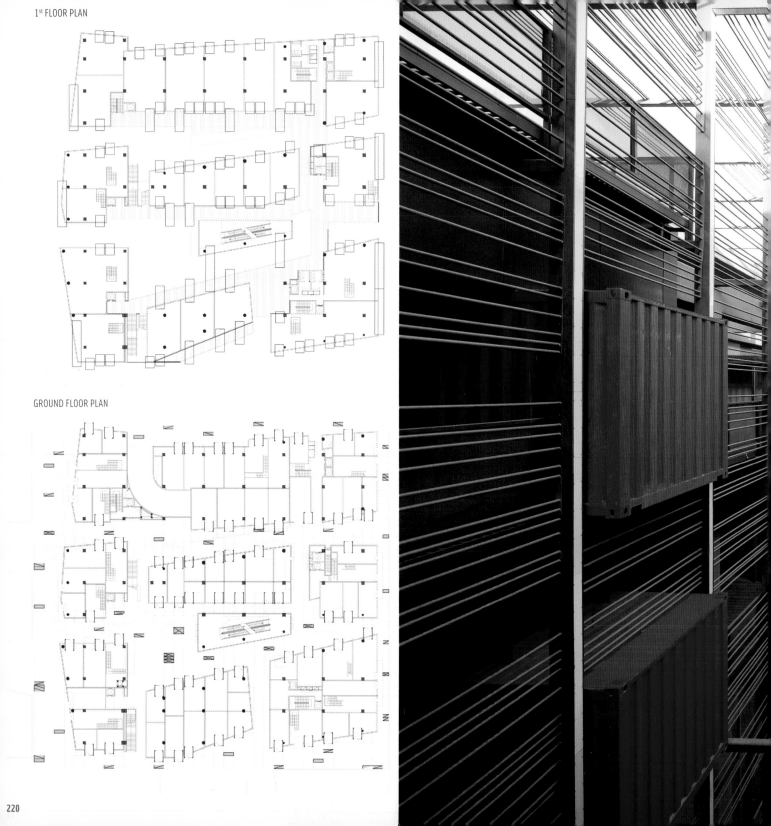

1ST FLOOR PLAN

GROUND FLOOR PLAN

Sanlitun Village is a mixed use development organized like a Medieval village, with a dense fabric of narrow alleys, low-rise buildings, elevated walkways and bridges connecting all levels. Located in Sanlitun, one of central Beijing busiest neighbourhoods undergoing very fast and radical transformation, the retail-and-office complex consists of four sections that were designed by four architects. The New York-based container architecture specialists LOT-EK were commissioned to create the north-east section comprised of three separate and interconnected buildings to be dedicated to retail, restaurants and event spaces.

Their concept derives from the old typology of the Chinese 'hutong', the internal urban alley animated by lively retail activity. LOT-EK have recreated this typography using a rhythmic system of scaffolding-like metal frames the width of a shipping container. Containers are inserted randomly into the façade of the building and jut out into the alleys. At ground level, containers serve as canopies that hover over the retail stores entrances and house display or other small programme on the interior. On the upper floors containers are pierced and skewered by the horizontal circulation functioning as entrances to the retail stores and as display windows along the loggias.

The scaffolding-like structure extends the alleys out towards the main street of the Sanlitun area to lure in passers-by. At every level the containers function as large three-dimensional graphic objects layered with signage and logos. Orange mesh, also pierced by shipping containers, wraps the external perimeter of the entire north-east section adding privacy and sun refraction along the outer façades.

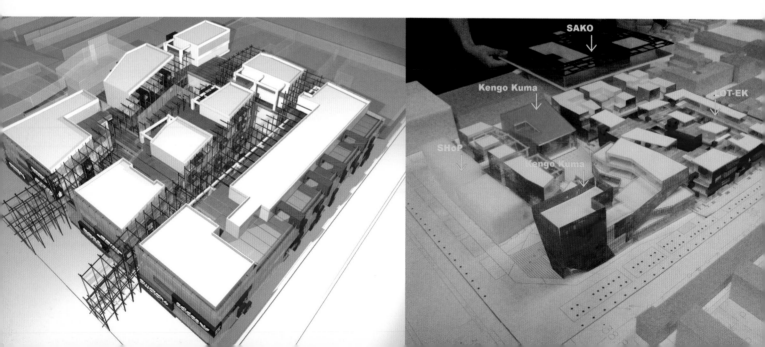

SAKO

Kengo Kuma

SHoP

Kengo Kuma

LOT-EK

2nd FLOOR PLAN

3th FLOOR PLAN

Maziar Behrooz
Container studio

location: **Arnagansett, New York, Usa**

use: **Art studio**

project year: **2009**

photography: **Francine Fleischer, Dalton Portella**

no. of containers: **2**

Dark charcoal on the outside and white passepartout on the inside, Container Studio is an art realm surrounded by a dense forest. It is a simple structure, both inviting and reflective.

Container Studio is an art studio in a forest in the state of New York. The client wanted it close to her house, so the studio and the house are on the same estate, and she needed it on the tight budget of $60,000.

The terrain has elevations, so Maziar Behrooz used two 40' shipping containers (cost: $2,500 each, delivered) and perched them over a 2.7 m (9') concrete foundation wall/cellar. By removing 75% of the containers' floors, the architect managed to unite the underground and ground level floor plans to create a large open atelier with a double-height ceiling, and thus overcome the prover- bial monotony of container constructions. With all the interior walls painted white, the studio looks spacious and inspiring. Large window cut outs flood the interior with daylight and enable the artist's visual communication with the natural surroundings, even from the painting studio at the lower level. Access to the painting studio on the lower level is via a wide staircase from the upper level. The staircase itself acts as a transitional space for viewing art work. The upper floor provides a more intimate work area and a sitting area. Entrance to the studio is from the upper level.

In contrast with the white passepartout interior, Container Studio's exterior was painted dark charcoal to maintain continuity with the original house, which Maziar Behrooz had renovated back in 2008, and to recede in the shadows of the densely wooded site.

GROUND FLOOR PLAN

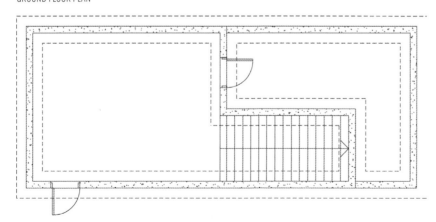

SECTION

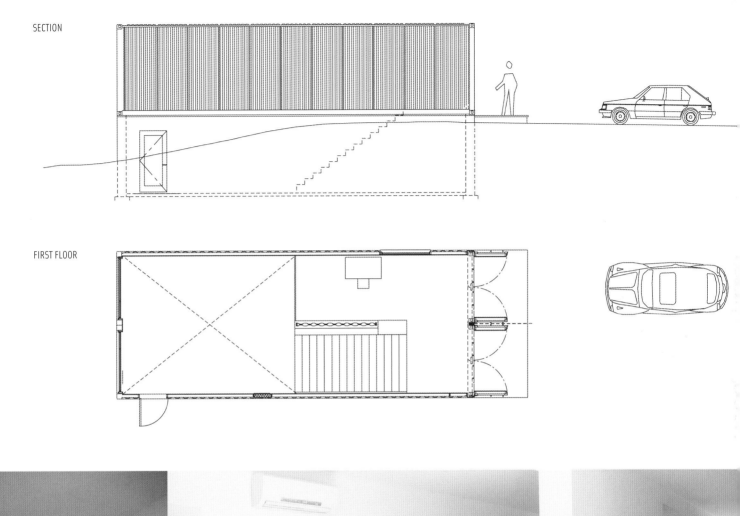

FIRST FLOOR

James & Mau architects
Infiniski
Manifesto House

location: **Curacavi, Chile**

use: **Single family home**

year of completion: **2009**

photography: **Antonio Corcuera**

no. of containers: **3**

An innovative and contemporary family home based on bioclimatic and modular architecture. Wearing a coat made of recycled transport pallets, it "breathes" with the seasons.

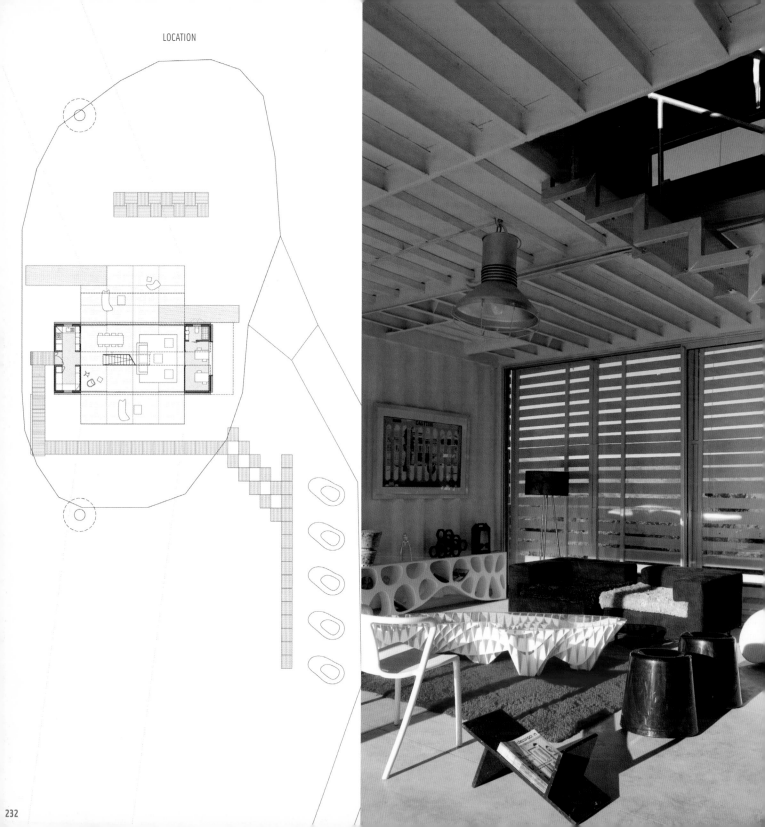

LOCATION

Like a mansion or a fortress, the Manifesto House is strategically perched on top of a hill enjoying a magnificent vista of the landscape below. Covering a total interior surface of 160 m2 (1,720 ft2), it houses a living room, kitchen and bathroom on the ground floor and master bedroom with two additional rooms upstairs.

The structure consists of three reused shipping containers. The container on the ground floor is divided into two separate parts that are set wide apart from each other and perpendicular to the two containers on top of them. This construction creates a large open space on the ground floor that is fully glazed to allow direct contact with nature and to flood the interior with daylight. Since the construction is wrapped in a wooden façade, its container origin remains hidden.

The house's signature design feature is its timber façade, which can be put on or taken off like a coat. On the one side it is made of horizontal wooden slats, while on the other it is composed of reused white transport pallets, which have, like containers, stepped out of the cargo/transport chain. The wooden façade also functions as a pergola.

The timber façade makes the house blend in more with its rural surroundings, while it also serves an important bioclimatic function. Depending on the weather and the season, the house puts its coat on or takes it off: in summertime, closed pergolas protect containers from overheating while allowing for maximum ventilation, and in wintertime the lifted pergolas let the sun in and allow for the greenhouse effect in the glazed interior. In addition to its bioclimatic design, which took account of the building's orientation, the direction of the wind and sun, the Manifesto House uses a series of other eco-friendly features, such as recycling (containers, pallets), reuse (construction materials), cut transport routes, integration of alternative and renewable energy (solar power), good insulation etc., which make the house almost 100% self-sufficient off grid.

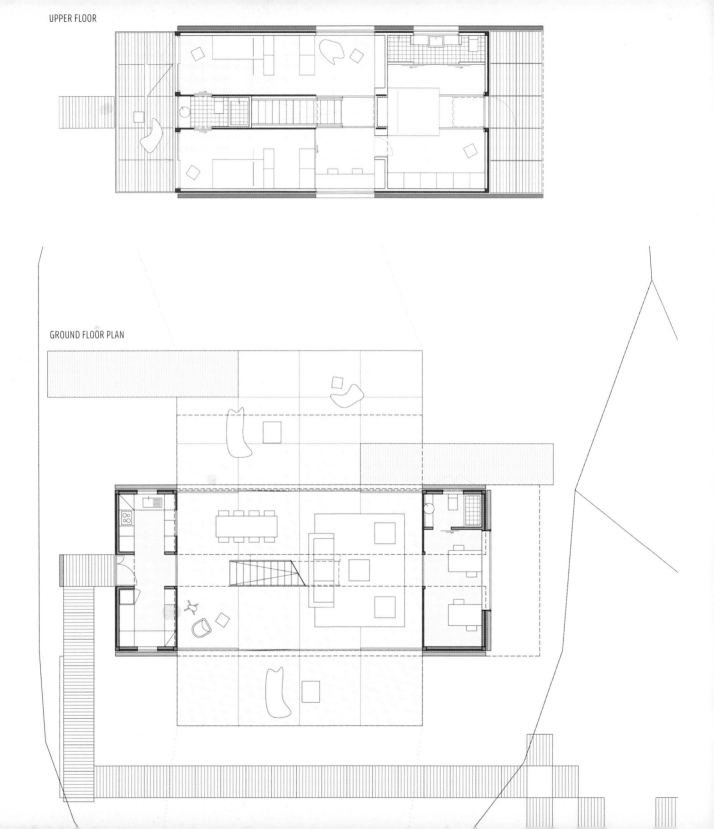

GROUND FLOOR PLAN

SECTIONS

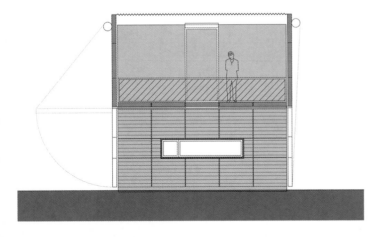

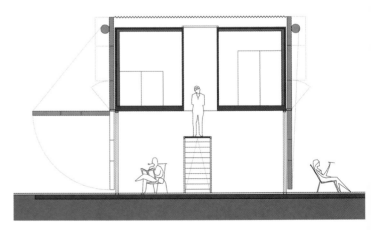

Robertson Design
Cordell House

location: **Houston, Texas, Usa**

use: **Family home**

year of completion: **2009**

photography: **Robertson Design**

no. of containers: **4**

Pulled out of the second largest cargo port in the US, four shipping containers in downtown Houston Texas have been reused and converted into a cosy and spacious family home.

Located in downtown Houston Texas, Cordell House is not far from the United States second largest port. Each year, more than 225 million tons of cargo pass through the 40 km (25 mi.) long port, including 1.6 million shipping containers – or 1.6 million potential building blocks, in the eyes of Houston developers Katie Nichols and John Walker.

Though containers are part of Houston's vernacular, Nichols and Walker knew the idea of living in one was not. So what they wanted to do was show that containers make for affordable yet design intensive housing. The challenge was to build a legitimately sellable container house by making it feel like a typical home.

Outside, the corrugated steel of three containers – two 40' modules and one 20' unit – form the northern, southern, and western facades of Cordell House, with a glass wall to the east completing the perimeter of the 3-bedroom home. Inside, the containers act as wide walls into which architect Christopher Robertson inserted the private and utility areas: the southern container houses the master suite, the northern one a bedroom and bath plus an opening for the office and playroom, while the 20' unit parallel to the street houses the kitchen and laundry rooms. In the middle, the dining room flows into the living, office and play spaces, then out the glass doors and onto the deck that connects the home to another 40' container, which houses the guest quarters and storage shed. The interiors are mainly white with warm complementary colours that, together with wooden floors, give the house a homey feel.

The corrugated steel of the containers has become a textured wall for writing messages and pinning up drawings. When the house was sold to a family of four, the parents felt bad at first because, as they were furnishing, they realised their fridge isn't magnetic for their children's artwork. Of course they soon realized the entire house is magnetic and drawings can be pinned up all over the house.

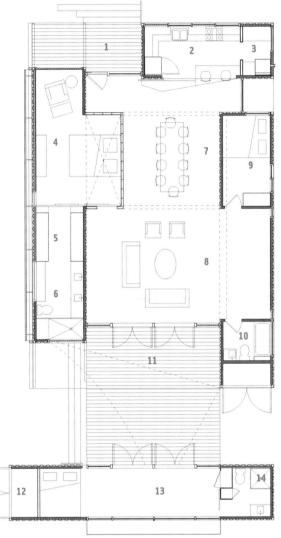

GROUND FLOOR PLAN

1. PORCH
2. KITCHEN
3. UTILITY
4. MASTER BEDROOM
5. MASTER CLOSET
6. MASTER BATHROOM
7. DINING
8. LIVING
9. BEDROOM
10. BATHROOM
11. PORCH
12. OUTDOOR STORAGE
13. GUEST QUARTERS
14. SHOWER

FAÇADE

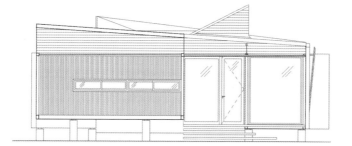

SECTIONS

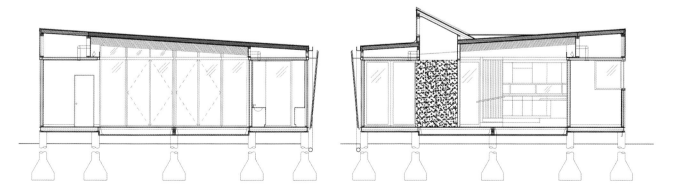

Ogrydziak
Prillinger architects
Triskelion

location: **San Francisco, California**

use: **Art gallery**

year of completion: **2010**

photography: **Tim Griffith**

no. of containers: **3**

The triangular composition of three containers and a space in between hides behind its steel façade a fabulous, spacious and well illuminated gallery.

Triskelion is a gallery located in the Presidio of San Francisco, a park on the northern tip of the San Francisco Peninsula, and hosts an exhibition of site-specific art. The structure is composed of three reclaimed shipping containers set at 120-degree angles relative to each other, and its north-facing wing is aligned to frame views of the nearby Golden Gate Bridge. The triangular space created at the centre of the arrangement supports a diffused skylight, acting as an atrium within the exhibition space for sculpture display. Thematising the temporary and mobile nature of the exhibition space, the overall form is a simple but innovative configuration of component parts that can be assembled and disassembled for use elsewhere. Each shipping container is painted to reflect the tricolour identity of the project sponsor, the FOR-SITE Foundation.

Designed for minimal impact on the existing site, the structure was manufactured off-site and trucked to location in four loads (three containers composing the structure proper and one extra container for additional smaller parts). The on-site fabrication was limited to the assembly of these primary components and the following three pieces: access path, deck, and a foundation system of twelve helical piers. Reinforced with minimal additional steel framing, the major components are bolted for assembly and disassembly. 100% daylight during normal operating hours, a photovoltaic array mounted on the roofs of the containers supplies the project's low-energy electrical needs. All additional elements on the site – access paths to negotiate site grades, a deck and outdoor benches, are constructed using reclaimed materials from the Presidio.

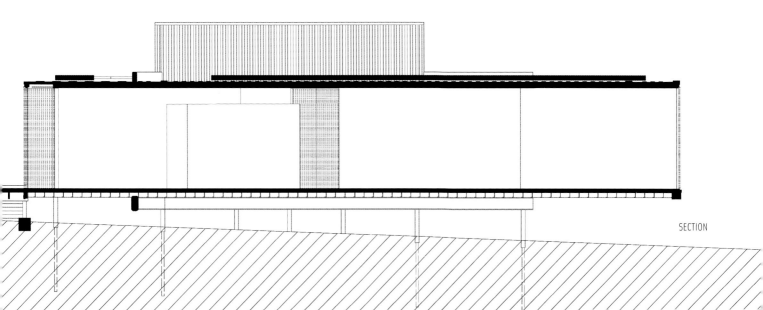

SECTION

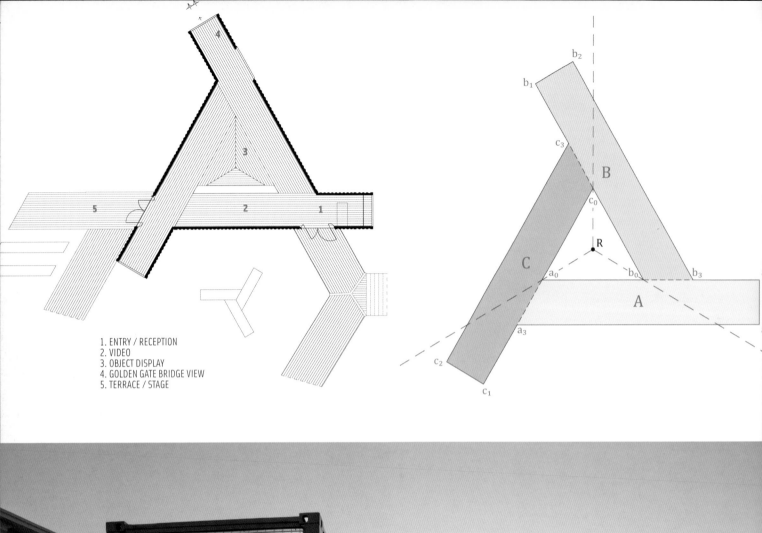

1. ENTRY / RECEPTION
2. VIDEO
3. OBJECT DISPLAY
4. GOLDEN GATE BRIDGE VIEW
5. TERRACE / STAGE

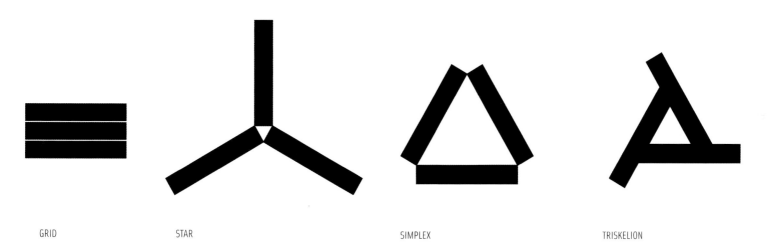

GRID

STAR

SIMPLEX

TRISKELION

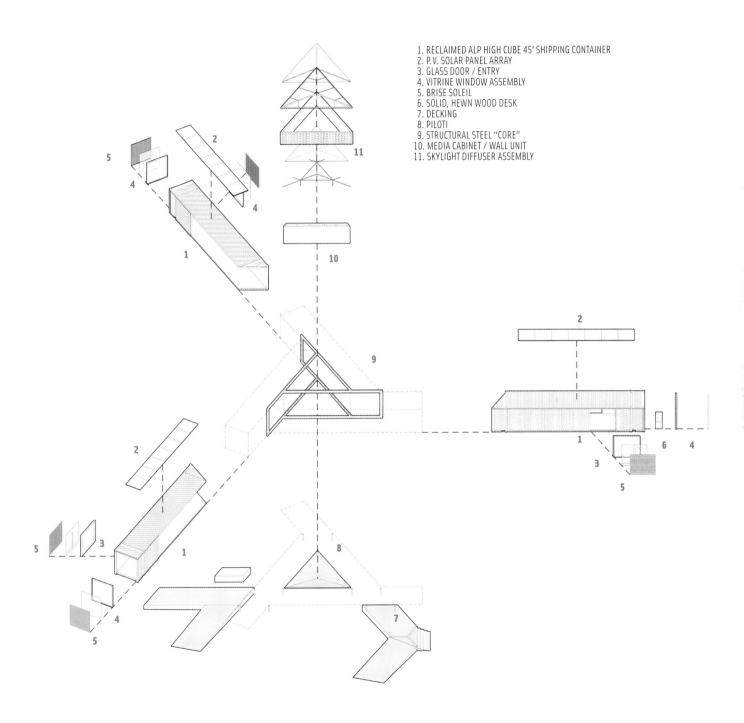

1. RECLAIMED ALP HIGH CUBE 45' SHIPPING CONTAINER
2. P.V. SOLAR PANEL ARRAY
3. GLASS DOOR / ENTRY
4. VITRINE WINDOW ASSEMBLY
5. BRISE SOLEIL
6. SOLID, HEWN WOOD DESK
7. DECKING
8. PILOTI
9. STRUCTURAL STEEL "CORE"
10. MEDIA CABINET / WALL UNIT
11. SKYLIGHT DIFFUSER ASSEMBLY

Ken Kwok
Upcycled container resort home

location: **Bukit Tinggi, Pahang, Malaysia**

use: **Weekend house**

year of completion: **2010**

photography: **Anand Bungalows SDN BHD**

no. of containers: **6**

Pulled out of the global cycle of trade, six upcycled shipping containers take on a nature-friendly coat and make a pleasant holiday retreat in a breathtaking natural environment.

FIRST FLOOR

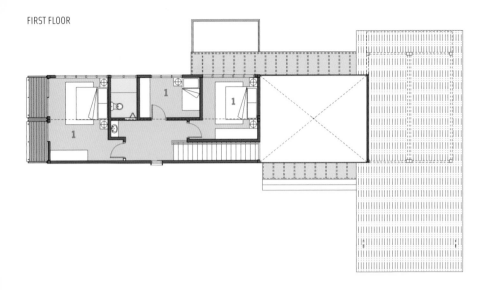

1. BEDROOM
2. KITCHEN
3. DINING ROOM
4. TERRACE
5. LIVING ROOM
6. ENTRANCE
7. MASTER BEDROOM
8. GARAGE

GROUND FLOOR

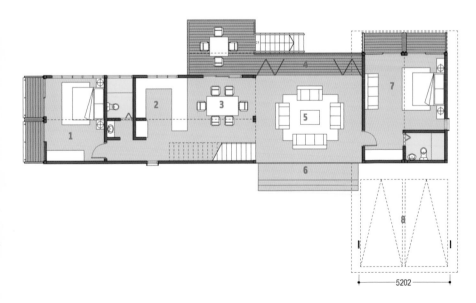

5202

Bukit Tinggi is a popular holiday area, with the surrounding native forest richly populated with a wide range of native species. ET Tan bought a plot on a steep sloping terrain there, looking to put up a weekend resort home there. And he wanted it fast. Fortunately he is a fan of container homes. Architect Ken Kwok set out to creating an up-cycled container home, which is not only cost-effective and was quick to assemble, but caused minimum site disruption and incorporates several eco-friendly features. The smart green home in Malaysia was constructed using the following principles: smart design, up-cycle & recycle, smart to build, energy efficiency and water conservation.

The frame structure consists of four 40' and two 20' containers. It is a big house, as Mr. Tan has a big family. It is a five-bedroom home with three bathrooms. The ground floor comprises a double volume living, dining and open kitchen area. Container doors were taken off and moved towards the inside, creating small balconies to gain extra space. Container walls form partitions between adjacent balconies, giving Mr. Tan's family members more privacy. The balconies not only act as a vertical motif of the façade but protect the interior from afternoon sun.

The north- and east-bound sides of the house have maximum fenestration for efficient use of daylight and natural ventilation. The building's orientation not only affords beautiful vistas of the natural surroundings, but takes advantage of the prevailing wind direction for good cross ventilation. The sun-exposed west and south facades have little fenestration to reduce heat load. No ceiling fan and air-conditioning is required for ventilation and no artificial lighting is needed for illumination during the day.

Project presentation

LONGITUDINAL FAÇADE

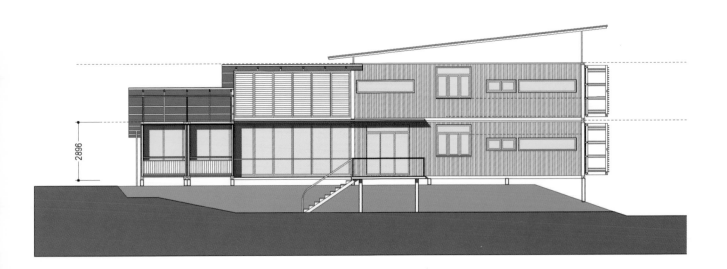

2896

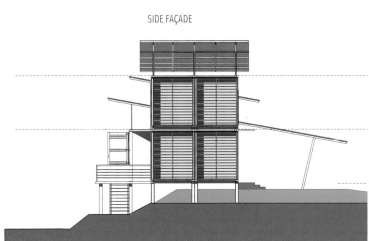

SIDE FAÇADE

Arhitektura
Jure Kotnik
Mobile Lighthouse Paris

use: **Lighthouse and promo gallery**

year: **2010**

location: **Paris, France**

collaborator: **Gerard Noirot/Seine 13**

photography: **Ports De Paris**

The mobile lighthouse which design connects two basic port elements, a traditional lighthouse and containers, was conceived to promote the sustainable fluvial transport and port activities on a various locations.

PORT DE LIMAY

GENNEVILIERS

Mobile lighthouse was designed to commemorate the 40th anniversary of the Paris port and to bring closer its activities to a broader audience. 'Port' is not something that most people would associate with Paris but with 20 million tons of cargo and 7 million people transported by water the port in Paris is the biggest inland port in France and second biggest in Europe. One of the aims of this lighthouse was a promotion of the fluvial transport as an environmental sustainable type of transport. Yearly transport on the rivers conducted by the port of Paris results in 1 million fewer trucks on the roads and a savings of 200 000 tons of Carbon Dioxide. The container mobile lighthouse was, symbolically as well as literally, illuminating this, enlightening visitors and to Paris and five different port locations along the rivers Seine and Marne (Ports of Evry, Limay, Paris, Gennevilliers and Bonneuil-sur-Marne) for a period of three months.

The design of the mobile lighthouse connects two basic port elements, a traditional lighthouse and containers. Lighthouses are one of most notable symbols of nautical transport and can be found in all traditional ports. Containers on the other hand are the symbol of the modern ports being a mainstay of goods transport. At the same time, they are a perfect material for constructing event architecture. They are accessible, allow mobility and are easily constructed and re-set again on some other location. Four recycled 20-foot containers form this 10 meter high lighthouse. The top container has two rotating beam headlights, while the ground floor container hosts an information office/gallery promoting port activities in the Paris region and river transport as an alternative to road transport.

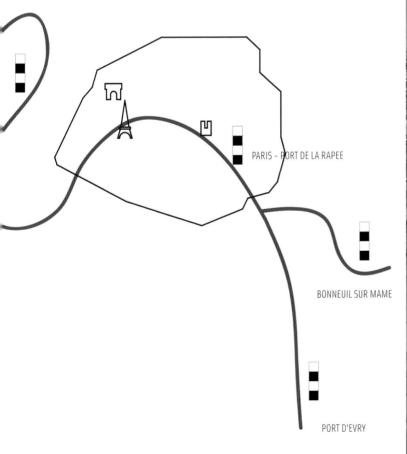

PARIS - PORT DE LA RAPEE

BONNEUIL SUR MAME

PORT D'EVRY

CONTMASTER

Kalmar

PARIS TERMINAL

PORTS de PARIS

1970 40 ans 2010
de transport fluvial en Île-de-France

PORTS de PARIS

www.1phare-sur-la-seine.com

Lighthouse Video

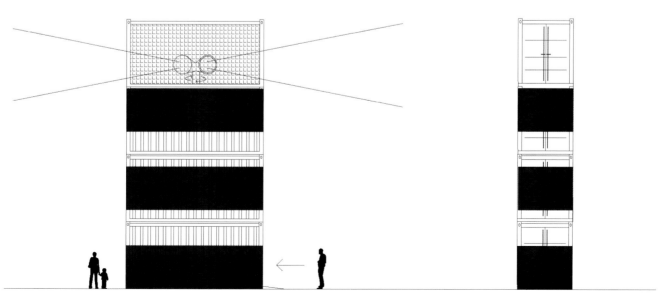

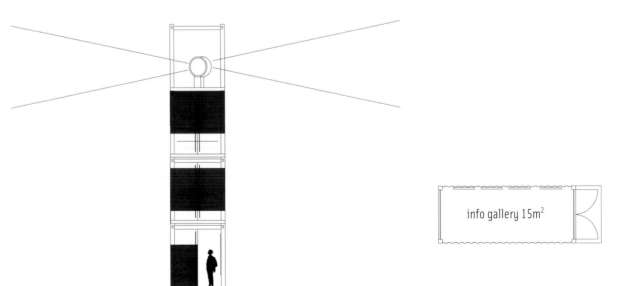

info gallery 15m²

ADITION

CONTAINERS

MOBILE LIGHTHOUSE

Cgarchitectes
Crossbox

location: **Pont Pean, France**

use: **Family home**

photography: **Javier Callegras**

no. of containers: **4**

By concealing its container origin on the inside as well as on the outside, Crossbox demonstrates the infinitely small difference that sets a container home apart from a typical prefab home.

GROUND FLOOR PLAN

1ST FLOOR PLAN

This stunning home in Brittany, France is located in a neighbourhood of contemporary-looking homes, in which it does not look conspicuous at all. But in fact it is quite unique: as opposed to the other houses there, it is composed from four 40' containers.

Containers are stacked crosswise on two levels. The perpendicular composition has several advantages, such as the top container projecting above the bottom one, sheltering the family car out front and providing shade at the back. The back garden is further animated by the swing attached to the overhanging bottom of the upper container.

The composition is simple and divided into two programme levels: the living area on the ground floor, and the less vibrant sleeping quarters on the first floor. The living area consists of a spacious living room, a kitchen and dining area, and washrooms. The top of the bottom container features a green roof at either end, which provides an extra planting space for the home. The upstairs floor plan reveals three bedrooms with a joint bath, which leads out onto the green roof. The other open terrace is accessible from the hall next to the staircase.

The interior of this modern residence is clad in a low-maintenance material for a sleek finish, simply furnished and bright. All evidence of the container origin of the house is gone, making it an acceptable living arrangement even for those that disfavour container homes.

This project does not capitalize on containers' trendy image but rather uses containers for the best of what they are: quality, low-cost, quick to assemble, easy to come by, and eco-friendly building blocks. Crossbox is the first realised container project, a showcase example, of an ambitious new series of family homes of various typographies, from single family homes to detached houses, based on container modules.

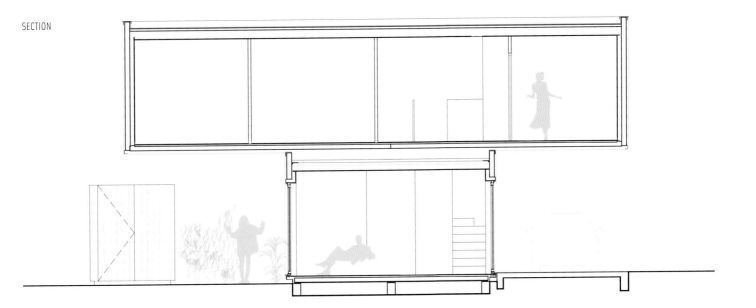

Sebastián Irarrázaval Arquitectos
Caterpillar House

location: **Santiago De Chile, Chile**

use: **Family Home**

year of completion: **2012**

photography: **Sebastián Irarrázaval Architects**

no. of containers: **12**

Caterpillar House stretches its limbs intuitively across the plane overlooking Chile's capital and is dynamically integrated into the landscape at the foothills of the Chilean Andes with which it forms an indivisible whole.

The map of international architecture has begun to include more and more Chilean authors. Quality design projects from Chile have increasingly been popping up over the last few years in particular, creating the image of this country being the architectural tiger of Latin America. Caterpillar House by Sebástian Irarrázaval is one stone in this booming and blossoming mosaic. Located in the mountainous outskirts of state capital Santiago de Chile, it offers breathtaking views of the city as well as of the surrounding mountains.

The dynamic structure consists of 12 containers of different sizes spread across two levels and integrated into the landscape at the foothills of the Andes. On the exterior containers are wrapped in a protective corten steel cladding, which makes the structure blend in with the sun-burnt environment and gives it an everlasting appearance.

The south facing tentacles of the building have large window openings to let in as much daylight as possible and offer unrestrained views of the city below. At the back of the building the tentacles bend upward, following the curve of the slope, and finish in skylights. Access to the house is from the upper level with the parking area, and communications are enabled through staircases housed inside steeply sloping containers. The upper floor accommodates six bedrooms with baths, while the lower floor is more vibrant in programme, hosting the kitchen, dining and living area within a single large open space. The different programmes can be separated with sliding partitions. The rough ceiling constructions are set against the background of gentle white walls and light grey flooring. This central area leads out onto the patio with a swimming pool cut out of a container shell.

Project video

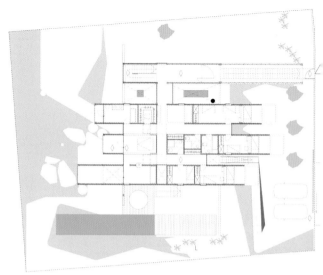

1ST FLOOR PLAN

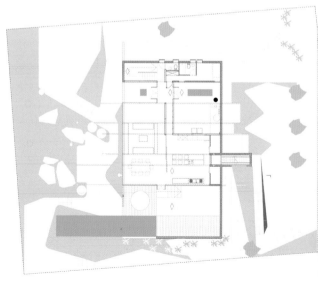

GROUND FLOOR PLAN

FAÇADES

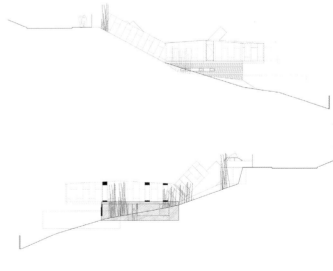

USM ltd.
Cubes

location: **Peaton Hill, Scotland, Uk**

use: **Artist Studios**

year of completion: **2002**

photography: **Nigel Reid Foster**

no. of containers: **6**

These artist retreat cabins blend in perfectly with the natural surroundings. The grass-covered roofs make the Cubes appear to be growing out of the slopes, with the glass fronts catching a reflection of the pond below and vice versa.

Cove Park is a center for established artists, situated on the west coast of Scotland on 50 acres of spectacular countryside. It supports the work of artists in residence, offering them a place of retreat and providing them with time, space and freedom to undertake significant research, develop their practice and ideas and/or create. The centre encompasses several accommodation facilities, including six en-suite accommodation units, known as Cubes, composed from the 20` container.

Although unusual for the rural surroundings, containers blend in perfectly. Cubes have been installed on a site overlooking Loch Long, an area of outstanding natural beauty. The grass-covered roofs make the Cubes' rear parts appear as if grown out of the slopes, with the glass fronts catching a reflection of the pond below and vice versa. Cubes have a dark green exterior with round windows typical of Container CityTM architecture.

A Cube is composed of two containers and has a kitchen/sitting area and a bath. Apart from one Cube, which has been fully equipped to accommodate the disabled and has a single bed, all the others have double beds. The fully glazed front sides overlooking the Loch invite plenty of daylight, so the insides are very bright. The feeling of brightness is reinforced by the white interior that contrasts vividly with the Cubes' colourful natural surroundings. Sliding glass doors lead out onto the decked balcony that runs along the front façade and extends over the pond, offering beautiful views of the Loch. Cubes are connected with each other with standard container doors, which give their residents privacy and independence.

PLANS

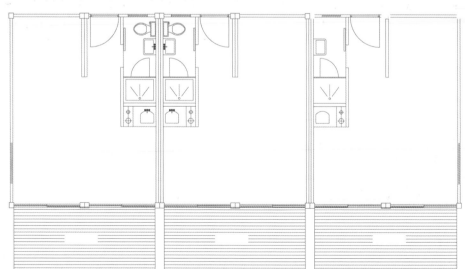

Shigeru Ban Architects
Nomadic Museum

location: **New York, USA, and other**

use: **Museum**

year of completion: **2005**

photography: **Michael Moran**

no. of containers: **148**

The atmosphere created by the paper tubes colonnade, stacks of steel containers and carefully directed light give the visitor the impression they are in a cathedral – a cathedral honoring art.

Gregory Colbert is the creator of Ashes and Snow, an exhibition of photographic artworks and films, who wanted his exhibition to tour the world in a mobile gallery or museum. He wanted something sustainable, innovative and fresh. Colbert wanted a cathedral for the 21st century and he got one – the Nomadic Museum.

This building's journey started on the abandoned Pier 54 of New York's Hudson River. Shigeru Ban created it from 148 borrowed cargo containers, stacked into a four-level self-supported grid. The open spaces between containers are secured with a diagonal tent-like fabric, creating the typical checkerboard pattern over the entire facade. The interior construction consists of triangular trusses of paper tubes resting on a colonnade of 11 m (36') high paper tube columns. A wooden walkway runs the length of the colonnade and is bordered on both sides by bays full of white-washed river stones, surrounding each column. Above these bays, large unframed photo artworks printed on hand-made Japanese paper are hung on thin cables, installed between the paper columns. This establishes a visual boundary between the physical space of the public walkway and the mystical domain of the images. The fact that shipping containers were used to make this monumental structure does not diminish the awe-inspiring experience of its interior.

Containers were chosen for the building because they are available everywhere the museum goes. Rather than having to ship the entire exhibit, only 37 containers have to be transported each time, to pack the fabric and materials for the structure. The remaining containers are borrowed on site. The Museum was so far erected in New York City, Santa Monica California and Tokyo, each time in a slightly different cast of containers, always adapting somewhat to its current environment.

Project video

PLAN

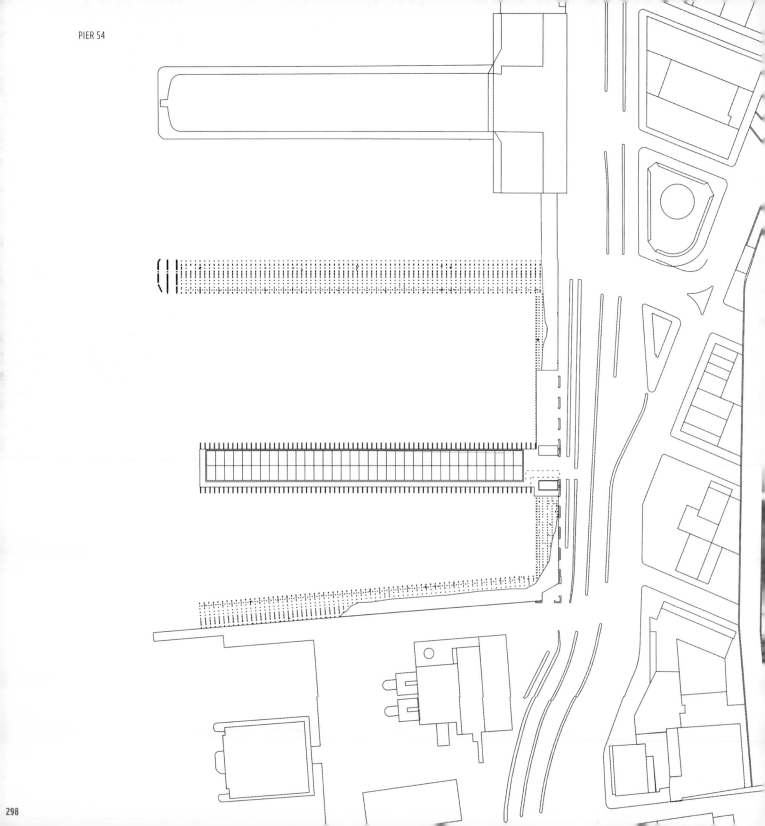

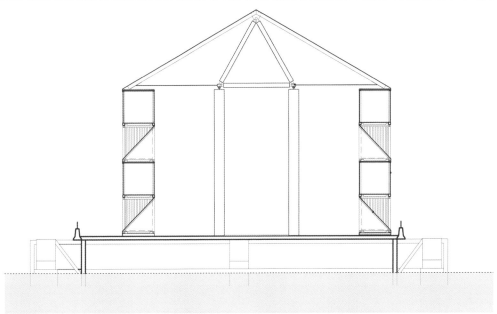

SECTION

* IPAD VERSION - APPLE STORE

BIBLIOGRAPHY:

Alter, L. (2011) Does shipping container architecture make sense?
[Online] Available: Treehugger, http://www.treehugger.com/modular-design/does-shipping-container-architecture-make-sense.html [28 Mar 2012]

Container Technology A-Z (2010) [e-book] **Cheyenne: GreenCube Network,**
http://www.trimo.eu/news/news-32/speech-by-professor-janez-kozelj-at-the-opening-of-the-first-exhibition-of-shipping-container-architecture/ [28 Mar 2012].

Jung, A. (2005) The Box That Makes the World Go Round, [Online] Available:
http://www.spiegel.de/international/spiegel/0,1518,386799,00.html [28 Mar 2012]

Kotnik, J. (2006) Konhiša : diplomska naloga. Ljubljana:Fakulteta za arhitekturo

Kotnik, J.(2008) Container architecture – this book contains 6,441 containers, Barcelona: LinksBooks*

Koželj, J. (2010), Opening speech at the World's first container architecture exhibition,
http://www.trimo.eu/news/news-32/speech-by-professor-janez-kozelj-at-the-opening-of-the-first-exhibition-of-shipping-container-architecture/ [21 Jun 2012],

Pagnotta, B. (2011) The pros and cons of cargo container architecture [Online], Available:
http://www.archdaily.com/160892/the-pros-and-cons-of-cargo-container-architecture/ [28 Mar 2012]

Slawik, H. Bergmann, J. Buchmeier, M., Slawik, H. (2010) Container Atlas: A Practical Guide to Container Architecture, Gestalten, Berlin

World Shipping Council [Online], Available:
http://www.worldshipping.org/about-the-industry/containers/global-container-fleet [28 Mar 2012]